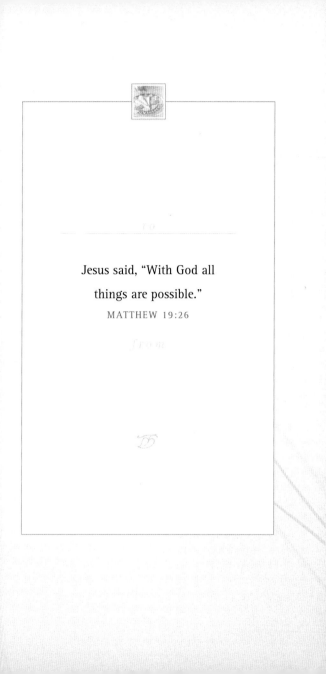

Jesus said, "With God all things are possible."

MATTHEW 19:26

God's Words of Life for Graduates
Copyright ©2004 by The Zondervan Corporation
ISBN 0-310-80365-9

Requests for information should be addressed to:
Inspirio, The gift group of Zondervan
Grand Rapids, Michigan 49530
http://www.inspirogifts.com

Editor: Janice Jacobson
Design Manager: Amy J. Wenger
Cover and Interior Design: Koechel Peterson and Associates
Compilers: Lee Stuart and Molly Detweiler

Printed in China
04 05 06/HK/ 4 3 2

God's Words of Life
for
Graduates

from the

New International Version

inspirio™

CONTENTS

Future Plans
(Yours and God's)

YOUR FUTURE RIGHT NOW probably looks a lot like a jungle. As you enter it, you feel excited, eager, and possibly a little lost. You don't know whether you have chosen the right trail, if you have the right tools and gear, or if the promised rewards really exist.

As you enter the jungle of your future, be wary: there are many treasures to be found, but only one is worth seeking—God's will for your life.

You must choose the right path by following God's lead. He is our guide through the jungle. He has provided us a guidebook, his Word. He has promised to lead us past the dangers of a world that honors what is worthless, and into his salvation.

May the LORD give you the desire of your heart and make all your plans succeed.

PSALM 20:4

It is God who works in you to will and
to act according to his good purpose.

PHILIPPIANS 2:13

*"I know the plans I have for you,"
declares the LORD, "plans to
prosper you and not to harm you,
plans to give you hope
and a future."*

JEREMIAH 29:11

*IN HIS HEART A MAN PLANS
HIS COURSE, BUT THE LORD
DETERMINES HIS STEPS.*

PROVERBS 16:9

IT IS WRITTEN:

*"No eye has seen,
   no ear has heard,
no mind has conceived
   what God has prepared for
   those who love him."*

1 CORINTHIANS 2:9

*Commit to the LORD whatever you do,
   and your plans will succeed.*

PROVERBS 16:3

Forgetting what is behind and straining toward what is ahead, I press on toward the goal to win the prize for which God has called me heavenward in Christ Jesus.

PHILIPPIANS 3:13–14

Now that you have graduated, everyone expects you to know what you'll be doing for the rest of your life. But you may not even know what you'll be doing next year!

Thinking of the future can be scary. But the fear is not necessary. God knows the desires of your heart and your uncertainties. And he promises not to leave you stranded without hope. You can relax in the knowledge that God has a unique plan for your life—a plan more fulfilling and a life more abundant than anything you could dream for yourself.

But his plan doesn't just happen by magic. You discover it as you draw closer to God each day. As you get to know him better and start making decisions affecting your future, his plans for your life are made clear. He guarantees it.

S. RICKLY CHRISTIAN

*Everything you
comprehend
through faith's
vision belongs
to you.*

Look as far as you can, for it is all
yours. Your world stands before you, filled
with limitless possibilities, wonderful
places to explore, and decisions to make every
day of your life. Do not look ahead to what
may happen tomorrow. The same everlasting
Father who cares for you today will take care
of you tomorrow and every day.

FRANCES DE SALES

*The plans of the LORD stand firm forever,
the purposes of his heart through all
generations.*

PSALM 33:11

Let love and faithfulness never leave you;
*   bind them around your neck,*
*   write them on the tablet of your heart.*
Then you will win favor and a good name
*   in the sight of God and man.*

PROVERBS 3:3–4

Plans fail for lack of counsel,
*   but with many advisers they succeed.*

PROVERBS 15:22

Whoever gives heed to instruction prospers,
*   and blessed is he who trusts in the LORD.*
The wise in heart are called discerning,
*   and pleasant words promote instruction.*

PROVERBS 16:20–21

The plans of the
diligent lead to profit.

PROVERBS 21:5

In your future plans, remember to first consult God—he is forming your life for your good and his glory.

You don't know what kinds of challenges you'll face next week, next month, next year. You don't know where your future will lead. But God does because he has scouted ahead.

"The Lord himself goes before you," the Bible says. God has seen what lies up the road. He has scouted the opposition, and he knows every obstacle, every rut and puddle that stands between you and ultimate victory.

S. RICKLY CHRISTIAN

Jesus said, "Surely I am with you always."

MATTHEW 28:20

When Doubts
Creep In ...

BEING RESTLESS AND HAVING worries are forbidden by our Lord. He said not to worry about what we shall eat or drink or wear (Matthew 6:31). He does not mean that we shouldn't think ahead or that our life should never have a plan or pattern. He simply means that we are not to worry about these things.

REV. DARLOW SARGEANT

Do not be anxious about anything, but in everything, by prayer and petition, with thanksgiving, present your requests to God. And the peace of God, which transcends all understanding, will guard your hearts and your minds in Christ Jesus.

PHILIPPIANS 4:6–7

The LORD lifted me out of the slimy pit,
    out of the mud and the mire;
He set my feet on a rock
    and gave me a firm place to stand.

PSALM 40:2

WHEN I SAID, "MY FOOT
IS SLIPPING,"
YOUR LOVE, O LORD,
SUPPORTED ME.

PSALM 94:18

"Though the mountains be shaken
    and the hills be removed,
yet my unfailing love for you will not be shaken
    nor my covenant of peace be removed,"
    says the LORD, who has compassion on you.

ISAIAH 54:10

When anxiety was great within me,
  your consolation brought joy to my soul,
  O Lord.

PSALM 94:19

The problems we fret most about are the very things we ought to trust God with. Nothing is too difficult for him. Release your grip on your worries now. For as Christ said, "What is impossible with men is possible with God."

S. RICKLY CHRISTIAN

Blessed is the man who trusts in the Lord,
  whose confidence is in him.

JEREMIAH 17:7

The Lord is my light and my salvation—
  whom shall I fear?

PSALM 27:1

Cast all your anxiety on God
because he cares for you.

1 PETER 5:7

Jesus said, "I tell you the truth, if you have faith and do not doubt, not only can you do what was done to the fig tree, but also you can say to this mountain, 'Go, throw yourself into the sea,' and it will be done."

MATTHEW 21:21

Do not fret because of evil men
   or be envious of those who do wrong;
for like the grass they will soon wither,
   like green plants they will soon die away.
Trust in the LORD and do good;
   dwell in the land and enjoy safe pasture.

PSALM 37:1–3

My heart is not proud, O LORD,
   my eyes are not haughty;
I do not concern myself with great matters
   or things too wonderful for me.
But I have stilled and quieted my soul.

PSALM 131:1–2

Between stubborn skepticism and
honest questioning, there is a huge gap,
and the disciple named Thomas dramatically
illustrated the difference. "Doubting Thomas"
is remembered for his practical honesty.
He never pretended; if he didn't know
something, he said so. If he felt discouraged,
he let it show.

When Thomas was told of Jesus' resurrection,
he insisted he needed to see the risen Lord for
himself—an event of such importance was too
great to take another's word for it.

Jesus honored this honest doubt by visiting
Thomas in person.

Thomas's questions and doubts led to a deeper
faith because they were sincerely expressed in
a genuine search for answers.

Think about areas in your life that make you feel like you're sliding backward. What do you think God is trying to teach you? When you walk with God, it doesn't matter if you're climbing up or sliding down—you will have equal growth in either direction. You will grow strong and brave and confident, and you will learn that allowing God control of your life makes the journey even more worthwhile.

I sought the LORD, and he answered me; he delivered me from all my fears.

Confronting Adversity

TIMES OF ADVERSITY CAN *feel like a desert: intense heat during sunlight hours, followed by frigid nights. It takes courage and endurance to traverse a desert. There aren't any good maps, no obvious paths to follow. You can feel lost, lonely, afraid. You don't know whether you'll be able to make it to the other side, back to happier times.*

But we all have to cross deserts in life ...

We must survive sandstorms of poor physical and emotional health.

We must refrain from running toward the mirages of unholy promises.

We must seek shelter after enduring the heat of making hard choices.

We must search for the oasis of God's love for us, the cool, forgiving, restful promise of His grace.

Only then will our journey through the desert be complete.

LEE STUART

The LORD is good, a refuge in times of trouble. He cares for those who trust in him.

NAHUM 1:7

I can do everything through God
who gives me strength.

PHILIPPIANS 4:13

God is our refuge and strength,
an ever-present help in trouble.
Therefore we will not fear, though the earth
give way and the mountains fall into
the heart of the sea,
though its waters roar and foam and the
mountains quake with their surging.

PSALM 46:1–3

WE SAY WITH CONFIDENCE,
"THE LORD IS MY HELPER;
I WILL NOT BE AFRAID,
WHAT CAN MAN DO TO ME?"

HEBREWS 13:6

Be strong in the Lord and
in his mighty power.

EPHESIANS 6:10

19

The events of our lives, when we let God use them, become the mysterious and perfect preparation for the work he has called us to.

BARBARA JOHNSON

Don't be fretful about the journey ahead; don't worry about where you are going or how you are going to get there. If you believe in the First Person of the Trinity, God the Father, also believe in the Second Person of the Trinity, the One who came as the Light of the World, not only to die for people, but to light the way. This One, Jesus Christ, is Himself the Light and will guide your footsteps along the way.

EDITH SCHAEFFER

*It is God who arms me with strength
    and makes my way perfect.
He makes my feet like the feet of a deer;
    he enables me to stand on the heights.*

2 SAMUEL 22:33–34

*My flesh and my heart may fail,
    but God is the strength of my heart
    and my portion forever.*

PSALM 73:26

We all

endure

sandstorms

in life ...

the frenzied, pelting, blinding storms of broken relationships, lost opportunities, and bad choices. Occasionally, we confront physical challenges—our health and well-being are tossed for a time. Sometimes,

we confront emotional challenges—our friends, our family, our schools, our jobs ... every "normal" part of life is blown off course.

In these times, we must be still, lay close to God, and listen to his heart. He may be using this storm to make us stronger.

LEE STUART

May our Lord Jesus Christ himself

and God our Father, who loved us

and by his grace gave us eternal

encouragement and good hope,

encourage your hearts and strengthen

you in every good deed and word.

2 THESSALONIANS 2:16–17

Why are you downcast, O my soul?
  Why so disturbed within me?
Put your hope in God,
  for I will yet praise him,
  my Savior and my God.

PSALM 42:11

*Failure doesn't get enough credit. It
teaches us humility, perseverance,
and the value of hard work. When
you fail, you have to learn from your
mistakes and move on. God gives you challenges in your life, but he gives them to you
for a reason. It's not like he's trying to hurt
you or punish you. He's giving you those challenges so you'll grow up and mature.*

DAVID ROBINSON,
PLAYER FOR THE SAN ANTONIO SPURS

*When I dwell on myself and my problems, my
troubles seem to grow. But when I dwell on
God, my troubles seem to go. That doesn't
mean things are always bright and rosy.
Christians aren't immune to hurt and
headache. Yet, God gives us a special capacity
to cope with such times.*

S. RICKLY CHRISTIAN

*My life philosophy in a nutshell is:
"Life is tough but God is faithful."*

SHEILA WALSH

If you're anything like me, you sometimes feel overwhelmed by the chaos of life and people around you. There are days when nothing or no one makes sense, and you're convinced you're the last surviving sane person. On days when I feel like that, it helps me to tell God and get the burden off my shoulders. That doesn't mean things will change overnight ... or necessarily at all. It just makes me feel better to know God understands how I feel.

S. RICKLY CHRISTIAN

Difficulties are opportunities for growth. How can we grow with no problems? The world is watching how the Christian acts under pressure. So don't be a pressure-filled bottle, but allow God to make something out of your problem. If we can stop complaining, we can start proclaiming what God is doing through our difficulties.

BARBARA JOHNSON

Making Wise
Choices

LIFE CAN GET CONFUSING *and conflicting.*
We have to decide what matters most or we
become victims of the loudest and latest
demands. We have the ability to discern
the difference between "good" and the "best."

Since we cannot do everything well, we
must carefully choose a few things on which
to concentrate. Our purpose for living should
be to bring honor to God rather than to bring
pleasure to ourselves. With that ideal in mind,
we can set our priorities by choosing what
will bring the greatest—and best—recognition
to God. If we do that, we'll be rich in
God's eyes.

Trust in the LORD with all your heart
*   and lean not on your own understanding;*
in all your ways acknowledge him,
*   and he will make your paths straight.*

PROVERBS 3:5-6

Your word is a
lamp to my feet
and a light for my
path, O LORD.

PSALM 119:105

*Every day of our lives we make choices about
how we're going to live. Wherever we find
ourselves in this fragile existence, we need to
be reminded that life can be brighter than
noonday and darkness like morning because
we are living fully in this moment, secure in
our hope in the Lord.*

WHETHER YOU TURN TO THE
RIGHT OR TO THE LEFT,
YOUR EARS WILL HEAR A
VOICE BEHIND YOU, SAYING,
"THIS IS THE WAY; WALK IN IT."

ISAIAH 30:21

"I will instruct you and

teach you in the way

you should go;

I will counsel you and

watch over you,"

says the LORD.

PSALM 32:8

The LORD will guide you always.

ISAIAH 58:11

To have a personal relationship with Jesus Christ has been phenomenal in my life. I often wonder why I make some decisions. Well, it's not me making them, but God is really taking control in my life and sort of steering me in the right direction when it comes time to make decisions.

BUCK WILLIAMS, FORMER NBA PLAYER

The world and its desires

pass away, but the man

who does the will of

God lives forever.

1 JOHN 2:17

If any of you lacks
wisdom, he should ask
God, who gives gener-
ously to all without
finding fault, and it will
be given to him.

JAMES 1:5

Wisdom is supreme; therefore get wisdom.
    Though it cost all you have, get understanding.

PROVERBS 4:7

Blessed is the man who finds wisdom,
    the man who gains understanding,
for she is more profitable than silver
    and yields better returns than gold.

PROVERBS 3:13–14

As we proceed down life's journey,
we can choose between two roads:
the road of this world's wisdom and
the road of God's wisdom.
The first leads us through deserts,
wastelands, and jagged mountains
of perplexity and frustration.
By contrast, the wisdom of
God takes us through the oasis
of understanding and the valley
of delight, leading us confidently
to fulfillment in this life
and the blessings of eternity.

TIM LAHAYE

The book of Proverbs explains how life works
most of the time. The godly, moral, hardwork-
ing, and wise will reap many rewards. Fools
and scoffers, though they may appear to be
successful, eventually will pay the cost of
their lifestyle.

Proverbs candidly concedes that the wise path
will not be the choice of many. It is easier to
live carelessly, but choices that seem right
may end up destroying you. However, those
who choose to follow God's path, outlined in
the book of Proverbs, will be safe, successful,
and come to know God himself.

For attaining wisdom and discipline;
*   for understanding words of insight;*
for acquiring a disciplined and prudent life,
*   doing what is right and just and fair;*
for giving prudence to the simple,
*   knowledge and discretion to the young—*
let the wise listen and add to their learning,
*   and let the discerning get guidance—*
for understanding proverbs and parables,
*   the sayings and riddles of the wise.*
The fear of the Lord *is the beginning of knowledge,*
*   but fools despise wisdom and discipline.*

PROVERBS 1:1–7

You Are
Outstanding!

outstanding at what you do? Here's some advice from Ben Carson, a "self-made" motivational counselor, neurosurgeon, and author of The Big Picture:

"If you recognize your talents, use them appropriately, and choose a field that uses those talents, you will rise to the top of your field. Thinking Big means opening our horizons, reaching for new possibilities in our lives, being open to whatever God has in store for us on the road ahead.

"Over the years I have urged others to give their best, to seek excellence, and to Think Big. One day I was mulling over those two words and I worked out an acrostic for it."

T   - Talent

H   - Honest

I   - Insight

N   - Nice

K   - Knowledge

B   - Books

I   - In-depth knowledge

G   - God

Write down the answers to these questions:

• What have I done well in so far?

_____

_____

_____

_____

• What do I like to do that has caused others
  to compliment me?

_____

_____

_____

_____

• What do I do well and think of as fun
  although my friends see it as work—or as
  a boring activity?

_____

_____

_____

_____

Each man has his own gift from God;
one has this gift, another has that.

1 CORINTHIANS 7:7

It is God who arms me with strength
and makes my way perfect.

PSALM 18:32

It was Christ who gave some to be apostles,
some to be prophets, some to be evangel-
ists, and some to be pastors and teachers,
to prepare God's people for works of serv-
ice, so that the body of Christ may be built
up until we all reach unity in the faith and
in the knowledge of the Son of God and
become mature, attaining to the whole
measure of the fullness of Christ.

EPHESIANS 4:11–13

Skill will bring success.

ECCLESIASTES 10:10

If it's

mediocrity

you're after,

it can be

had easily.

But if you are to attain excellence, no matter what the field, you must work with all your might. You can't be allergic to sweat. You must also, on occasion at least, thumb your nose at the skeptics around you. They've been wrong before and they'll be wrong again.

S. RICKLY CHRISTIAN

Just as you excel in everything—in faith, in speech, in knowledge, in complete earnestness and in your love for us—see that you also excel in this grace of giving.

2 CORINTHIANS 8:7

Whatever is true, whatever is noble, whatever is right, whatever is pure, whatever is lovely, whatever is admirable—if anything is excellent or praiseworthy—think about such things.

PHILIPPIANS 4:8

*Achievements of great worth
and importance are not
accomplished without patient
perseverance and a considerable
interval of time. For as the saying
goes, "Rome was not built in a day."*

E. COBHAM BREWER

Let us not become weary in doing good, for at

the proper time we will reap a harvest if we

do not give up.

GALATIANS 6:9

*Our light and momentary troubles
are achieving for us an eternal glory
that far outweighs them all.*

2 CORINTHIANS 4:17

*Do not throw away your confidence;
it will be richly rewarded. You need to
persevere so that when you have done the will
of God, you will receive what he has promised.
For in just a very little while,
    "He who is coming will come and will not delay."*

HEBREWS 10:35–37

Blessed is the man who perseveres under

trial, because when he has stood the test,

he will receive the crown of life that God

has promised to those who love him.

JAMES 1:12

Jesus said, "To him who overcomes,
I will give the right to sit with me
on my throne, just as I overcame
and sat down with my Father
on his throne."

REVELATION 3:21

*May the LORD direct your hearts into God's
love and Christ's perseverance.*

2 THESSALONIANS 3:5

Have Courage!

COURAGE AND FEAR ARE *strange bedmates.*
It would seem to be impossible to have one
and have the other, too, and yet I believe that
is the challenge of the Christian life. Courage
and fear belong together. Fear tells us that
life is unpredictable, that anything can
happen. Courage replies quietly, "Yes,
but God is in control."

SHEILA WALSH

Be strong and courageous.

Do not be terrified; do not

be discouraged, for the

LORD your God will be with

you wherever you go.

JOSHUA 1:9

Do not fear, for I am with you;
do not be dismayed, for I am your God.
I will strengthen you and help you;
I will uphold you with my righteous right hand.

ISAIAH 41:10

> *WAIT FOR THE LORD;*
> *BE STRONG AND TAKE HEART*
> *AND WAIT FOR THE LORD.*
>
> PSALM 27:14

Do not be afraid. Stand firm
and you will see the deliverance
the LORD will bring you today.

EXODUS 14:13

Even youths grow tired
and weary ... but those who
hope in the LORD will renew
their strength. They will soar
on wings like eagles; they will
run and not grow weary, they
will walk and not be faint.

ISAIAH 40:30–31

The LORD himself goes before you and will be with you; he will never leave you nor forsake you. Do not be afraid; do not be discouraged.

DEUTERONOMY 31:8

The LORD is my strength and my shield;
my heart trusts in him, and I am helped.

PSALM 28:7

With your help I can advance against a troop;
with my God I can scale a wall.

PSALM 18:29

"Fear not, for I have redeemed you;
I have summoned you by name; you are mine," says the LORD.

ISAIAH 43:1

I lie down and sleep;
I wake again, because
*the L*ORD *sustains me.*
I will not fear the tens
of thousands drawn
up against me on
every side. ...
*From the L*ORD *comes*
deliverance.

PSALM 3:5–6, 8

Even though I walk
through the valley of the shadow of death,
I will fear no evil,
for you are with me;
your rod and your staff,
they comfort me.

PSALM 23:4

When I am afraid,
I will trust in you.
In God, whose word I praise,
in God I trust; I will not be afraid.
What can mortal man do to me?

PSALM 56:3–4

Thanks be to God! He gives
us the victory through
our Lord Jesus Christ.

1 CORINTHIANS 15:57

*We face pressures and struggles
every day. But we have found a way
to deal with them and live through
them—with God's help—and you can,
too. We can be on the path to victory,
if we trust God with our lives.*

JOHN SMOLTZ, ATLANTA BRAVES PITCHER

*You give me your shield of victory, LORD,
and your right hand sustains me;
you stoop down to make me great.*

PSALM 18:35

*God holds victory in store for the upright,
he is a shield to those whose walk is blameless.*

PROVERBS 2:7

The LORD your God is the one who goes with you to fight for you against your enemies to give you victory.

DEUTERONOMY 20:4

Everyone born of God overcomes the world. This is the victory that has overcome the world, even our faith. Who is it that overcomes the world? Only he who believes that Jesus is the Son of God.

1 JOHN 5:4–5

With God we will gain the victory.

PSALM 60:12

Having Faith

WITHOUT FAITH IT IS impossible to please God, because anyone who comes to him must believe that he exists and that he rewards those who earnestly seek him.

HEBREWS 11:6

Faith resembles a difficult race. The runner has his or her eyes on the winner's prize, and despite nagging temptations to slacken the pace, refuses to let up until crossing the finish line. Faith is like that ... a constant commitment to hang on and believe in God against all odds.

Just being alive in this fast-paced, challenging world requires faith and courage. Often, we don't recognize our own courage, our everyday acts of faith. Today, notice how often you speak out in a meeting, make time to go to the gym, or send a note to someone who needs a little support. These little acts of faith help you get closer to God.

*Faith comes from hearing
the message, and the message is
heard through the word of Christ.*

ROMANS 10:17

> *FAITH IS BEING SURE OF
> WHAT WE HOPE FOR AND
> CERTAIN OF WHAT WE
> DO NOT SEE.*
>
> HEBREWS 11:1

Since we have confidence to enter the Most
Holy Place by the blood of Jesus, by a new
and living way opened for us through the
curtain, that is, his body, and since we have a
great priest over the house of God, let us draw
near to God with a sincere heart in full
assurance of faith, having our hearts sprinkled
to cleanse us from a guilty conscience and
having our bodies washed with pure water.

HEBREWS 10:19–22

We live by faith, not by sight.

2 CORINTHIANS 5:7

*The only thing that counts is
faith expressing itself through love.*

GALATIANS 5:6

*The life of faith is a long, tough climb.
But it is filled with beauty if your eyes are
open to it. There's beauty in every step, in
every pause, in every struggle. Strive for
the summit, but cherish the process of
reaching it.*

*In talking about the Christian faith, the
writers of the Bible used hard words like
"struggle," "race," and "battle." They were
saying it's not easy to be a Christian in a
non-Christian world. Even faith is not easy.
When Christ said your faith could move
mountains, he didn't mean it was as simple as saying, "Presto-Chango!" He meant
that faith that moves mountains always
carries a pick.*

S. RICKLY CHRISTIAN

The testing of your faith develops perseverance.

Perseverance must finish its work so that you may be mature and complete, not lacking anything.

JAMES 1:4

Put your faith to the test by getting involved in people's lives. Don't just pray for others; roll up your sleeves and help them. Anyone can say they believe. But how many are willing, for example, to spend time with an unpopular person whom others ignore? Your faith and love for God ought to motivate you to love others actively and practically. Faith like that speaks louder than words.

S. RICKLY CHRISTIAN

"Have faith in God," Jesus said. "I tell you the truth, if anyone says to this mountain, 'Go throw yourself into the sea,' and does not doubt in his heart but believes that what he says will happen, it will be done for him. Therefore, I tell you, whatever you ask for in prayer, believe that you have received it, and it will be yours."

MARK 11:22-24

Take up the shield of faith,
with which you can
extinguish all the flaming
arrows of the evil one.

EPHESIANS 6:16

[Trials] have come so that your faith—of greater worth than gold, which perishes even though refined by fire—may be proved genuine and may result in praise, glory and honor when Jesus Christ is revealed. Though you have not seen him, you love him; and even though you do not see him now, you believe in him and are filled with an inexpressible and glorious joy, for you are receiving the goal of your faith, the salvation of your souls.

1 PETER 1:7–9

Faith is the wire that connects
you to grace, and over which
grace comes streaming from God.

ANONYMOUS

In Christ and through faith in
him we may approach God with
freedom and confidence.

EPHESIANS 3:12

In the gospel a righteousness from God is
revealed, a righteousness that is by faith
from first to last, just as it is written: "The
righteous will live by faith."

ROMANS 1:17

It is by grace you have been
saved, through faith—and this
not from yourselves, it is
the gift of God.

EPHESIANS 2:8

I pray that out of his glorious riches he may
strengthen you with power through his Spirit
in your inner being, so that Christ may dwell
in your hearts through faith.

EPHESIANS 3:16-17

Life with Friends

A STORY IS TOLD ABOUT *a little boy who,*
valiantly but unsuccessfully, tried to move
a heavy log. The boy's father stood nearby,
watching his son strain against the load.
Finally, he said, "Son, why aren't you
using all of your strength?"
Confused and angry, the boy said, "Dad, I'm
using every last bit of strength I have!"
"No, son, you're not," said the father. "You
haven't asked me to help."
Use every strength—every friend—you have.

A friend loves at all times,
and a brother is born for adversity.

PROVERBS 17:17

Dear friends, let us love one another,
for love comes from God. Everyone
who loves has been born of God and
knows God.

1 JOHN 4:7

How good and pleasant it is
when brothers live together in unity!

PSALM 133:1

Be devoted to one another in brotherly love.
Honor one another above yourselves.

ROMANS 12:10

Encourage one another and build each other
up, just as in fact you are doing.

1 THESSALONIANS 5:11

TWO ARE BETTER THAN ONE,
BECAUSE THEY HAVE A
GOOD RETURN FOR THEIR
WORK: IF ONE FALLS DOWN,
HIS FRIEND CAN HELP HIM UP.

ECCLESIASTES 4:9–10

If we walk in the light, as

God is in the light, we have

fellowship with one another.

1 JOHN 1:7

*Above all, love each other deeply,
because love covers a multitude of sins.*

1 PETER 4:8

*Look around. Who's there for you? And
who are you there for? Take a careful look.
Even those who insist they can make it on
their own may just be waiting for you to
reach out and help. Be there and available.*

LUCI SWINDOLL

Let us not give up meeting
together, as some are in
the habit of doing, but
let us encourage one another.

HEBREWS 10:25

*There is a friend who sticks
closer than a brother.*

PROVERBS 18:24

As we have opportunity,
let us do good to all people, especially to those
who belong to the family
of believers.

GALATIANS 6:10

*A despairing man should have
the devotion of his friends.*

JOB 6:14

*My intercessor is my friend
as my eyes pour out tears to God;
on behalf of a man he pleads with God
as a man pleads for his friend.*

JOB 16:20-21

*We should never complain that
our lives are hard while we know
that Jesus is our friend.*

ANONYMOUS

Strong friendships almost always involve self-sacrifice. People who don't wish to be inconvenienced or embarrassed or deal with a long, long list of other impositions and annoyances don't usually endure. Almost every human relationship is messy once in awhile. Being a real friend means giving freely and expecting nothing in return. That's the Christ model!

PEGGY BENSON

Perfume and incense bring joy to the heart, and the pleasantness of one's friend springs from his earnest counsel.

PROVERBS 27:9

Jesus said, "Greater love has no one than this, that he lay down his life for his friends. You are my friends if you do what I command. I no longer call you servants, because a servant does not know his master's business. Instead, I have called you friends, for everything that I learned from my Father I have made known to you. You did not choose me, but I chose you and appointed you to go and bear fruit—fruit that will last. Then the Father will give you whatever you ask in my name."

JOHN 15:13–16

Carry each other's burdens, and in this way you will fulfill the law of Christ.

GALATIANS 6:2

A true friend is a gift of God.

ROBERT SOUTH

Love one another deeply, from the heart.

1 PETER 1:22

Building Character

CHARACTER IS NOT A MATTER *of outward technique but of inner reality. It's amazing what God can do with a person who wants to grow personally and develop character. The great news is that God wants us to grow as much as we can. He redeemed us for that purpose. God wants to help us to develop our character.*

Your attitude should be the same as that of
Christ Jesus: Who, being in very nature God,
did not consider equality with God some-
thing to be grasped,
but made himself nothing,
taking the very nature of a servant,
being made in human likeness.
And being found in appearance as a man,
he humbled himself
and became obedient to death —
even death on a cross!
Therefore God exalted him to the highest place
and gave him the name that is above every name,
that at the name of Jesus every knee should bow,
in heaven and on earth and under the earth,
and every tongue confess that Jesus Christ is Lord
to the glory of God the Father.

PHILIPPIANS 2:5–11

The character trait that best enables us
to live a life worthy of Christ is humility.
In his earthly life, Christ was the perfect
example of true humility.

This trait has fallen on hard times.
Contrary to popular opinion,
humility is not a matter of
weakness; it is actually disciplined
strength and putting others first.
The problem with the virtue of
humility is that as soon as we
think we have attained it,
we have lost it. Jesus set the
perfect example. We should seek
to follow his lead in demonstrating
the kind of humility that will
cause others to see Jesus in us.

> HUMBLE YOURSELVES
> BEFORE THE LORD, AND HE
> WILL LIFT YOU UP.
>
> JAMES 4:10

Jesus said, "Everyone who exalts

himself will be humbled, and he who

humbles himself will be exalted."

LUKE 18:14

A man's pride brings him low,
  but a man of lowly spirit gains honor.

PROVERBS 29:23

His divine power has given us
everything we need for life and godliness
through our knowledge of him who
called us by his own glory and goodness.
... For this very reason, make every effort
to add to your faith goodness; and to
goodness, knowledge; and to knowledge,
self-control; and to self-control, perseverance; and to perseverance, godliness; and
to godliness, brotherly kindness; and to
brotherly kindness, love.

2 PETER 1:3, 5-7

Blessed is the man
  who does not walk in the counsel of the wicked
or stand in the way of sinners
  or sit in the seat of mockers.
But his delight is in the law of the Lord,
  and on his law he meditates day and
  night.

PSALM 1:1-2

As God's chosen people,

holy and dearly loved,

clothe yourselves with

compassion, kindness,

humility, gentleness

and patience.

COLOSSIANS 3:12

LORD, who may dwell in your sanctuary?
  Who may live on your holy hill?
He whose walk is blameless
  and who does what is righteous,
who speaks the truth from his heart
  and has no slander on his tongue,
who does his neighbor no wrong
  and casts no slur on his fellowman,
who despises a vile man
  but honors those who fear the LORD,
who keeps his oath even when it hurts,
  who lends his money without usury
and does not accept a bribe against the innocent.
  He who does these things will never be
  shaken.

PSALM 15:1–5

He has showed you, O man, what is good.
  And what does the LORD require of you?
To act justly and to love mercy
  and to walk humbly with your God.

MICAH 6:8

The Apostle Paul compares the Christian life to a race. Every Christian is called to run this race. It begins the moment we commit our lives to Christ, and it will conclude at the moment of death. Everything in life between these two moments is the race God has set before us.

We must run God's race to win. We must press on to win the heavenly crown. The essentials for winning the Christian race are self-discipline, determination, concentration, perseverance, dedication, and the will to win. These are the character qualities that lead to victory in God's race—the race of faith.

TOM LANDRY,
FORMER COACH OF THE DALLAS COWBOYS

We also rejoice in our sufferings,
because we know that suffering produces
perseverance; perseverance, character;
and character, hope. And hope does not
disappoint us, because God has poured out
his love into our hearts by the Holy Spirit,
whom he has given us.

ROMANS 5:3–5

Keep your father's commands
*   and do not forsake your mother's teaching.*
Bind them upon your heart forever;
*   fasten them around your neck.*
When you walk, they will guide you;
*   when you sleep, they will watch over you;*
*   when you awake, they will speak to you.*
For these commands are a lamp,
*   this teaching is a light,*
and the corrections of discipline
*   are the way to life,*

PROVERBS 6:20–23

Integrity:
A "True-North Compass"

A COMPASS NEEDLE ALWAYS *points north.
From it you can get your bearings...even
when the trail isn't marked and the path is
hard to follow.*

*Just as a compass needle points north, the
Bible always points to God. When we're lost in
the dark paths of life, it points us to the truth,
to the light of God's will. Every day we face
worries and temptations. We have to make
important decisions that will challenge our
values, our honesty, and our integrity ...
decisions that will set a course for the rest
of our lives.*

*A compass isn't much good if you don't trust
it and follow its direction. Likewise, knowledge
of the Bible is great, but if you don't trust it
and obey what it says, you'll still be lost in the
dark. God's words are different from the
words in any other book you'll ever read.
The Bible points from the darkness to the
light, from death to life! It always points
"true north."*

I strive always
to keep my
conscience clear
before God
and man.

ACTS 24:16

The LORD delights in men
who are truthful.

PROVERBS 12:22

TO DO WHAT IS RIGHT
AND JUST IS MORE
ACCEPTABLE TO THE
LORD THAN SACRIFICE.

PROVERBS 21:3

Jesus said, "In everything,
do to others what you
would have them do to
you, for this sums up the
Law and the Prophets."

MATTHEW 7:12

*We are taking pains to do what is right,
not only in the eyes of the Lord but
also in the eyes of men.*

2 CORINTHIANS 8:21

*The man of integrity walks securely,
but he who takes crooked paths will be
found out.*

PROVERBS 10:9

*Let us not become weary in
doing good, for at the proper
time we will reap a harvest
if we do not give up.*

GALATIANS 6:9

*Discretion will protect you,
and understanding will guard you.*

PROVERBS 2:11

I know, my
God, that you
test the heart
and are
pleased with
integrity.

1 CHRONICLES
29:17

*Those who have trusted
in God [must] be careful
to devote themselves to
doing what is good.*

TITUS 3:8

*A man's ways are in full view of the LORD,
and he examines all his paths.*

PROVERBS 5:21

*The Biblical virtue of integrity points to a
consistency between what is inside and what
is outside, between belief and behavior, our
words and our ways, our attitudes and our
actions, our values and our practices. Let
your personal commitment to integrity show
in what you do every day. As you do so,
you'll become a person whom others will
eagerly follow.*

*Every person should periodically ask himself,
"Do I have a price?" A faithful person's
commitment to God should be such that he or
she will obey him no matter what he or she is
asked to compromise. So ask yourself, "What
is my price? What would it take for me to
disobey God?" Rock-solid, non-negotiable
commitment is a crucial element of integrity.*

May integrity and uprightness protect me,
because my hope is in you, O LORD.

PSALM 25:21

Above all else, guard your heart,
for it is the wellspring of life.

PROVERBS 4:23

The righteous will flourish like a palm tree,
they will grow like a cedar of Lebanon;
planted in the house of the LORD,
they will flourish in the courts of our God.
They will still bear fruit in old age,
they will stay fresh and green,

PSALM 92:12–14

Truthful lips endure forever,
  but a lying tongue lasts only a moment.

PROVERBS 12:19

Do your best to present yourself to
God as one approved, a workman
who does not need to be ashamed
and who correctly handles
the word of truth.

2 TIMOTHY 2:15

Speaking the truth in love,
we will in all things grow up
into him who is the Head,
that is, Christ.

EPHESIANS 4:15

Success, Money, and Rewards

IN TODAY'S WORLD, IT IS *easy to be moti-vated and tempted by ambition, by a quest for material rewards, and by a preoccupation with "status." If we're not careful, we can succumb to running a race toward wealth and falling out of step with what really matters.*

As followers of Christ, the motive that drives us to excellence and success should be a desire to please the one who will give us our final reward. Everything we do should be done with a conscious awareness of his presence, a real-ization that he is watching. Such awareness should cause us to give our best effort all the time, knowing there is never a time when the one we follow is not with us, urging us on to our best.

> The LORD rewards
> every man for his
> righteousness and
> faithfulness.
>
> 1 SAMUEL 26:23

Do you not know that in a race all the runners run, but only one gets the prize? Run in such a way as to get the prize. Everyone who competes in the games goes into strict training. They do it to get a crown that will not last; but we do it to get a crown that will last forever.

1 CORINTHIANS 9:24–25

WHAT DOES THE BIBLE SAY ABOUT MONEY AND AVOIDING GREED?

Command those who are rich in this present world not to be arrogant nor to put their hope in wealth, which is so uncertain, but to put their hope in God, who richly provides us with everything for our enjoyment. Command them to do good, to be rich in good deeds, and to be generous and willing to share. In this way they will lay up treasure for themselves as a firm foundation for the coming age, so that they may take hold of the life that is truly life.

1 TIMOTHY 6:17–19

Keep your lives free from the love of money
and be content with what you have, because
God has said:
"Never will I leave you;
never will I forsake you."

HEBREWS 13:5

Jesus said, "Watch out! Be on
your guard against all kinds of
greed; a man's life does not
consist in the abundance
of his possessions."

LUKE 12:15

Keep falsehood and lies far from me;
give me neither poverty nor riches,
but give me only my daily bread.
Otherwise, I may have too much and
disown you and say,
"Who is the Lord?"
Or I may become poor and steal,
and so dishonor the name of my God.

PROVERBS 30:8-9

> *The LORD
> is my
> shepherd,
> I shall
> not be
> in want.*
>
> PSALM 23:1

I know what it is to be in need, and I know what it is to have plenty. I have learned the secret of being content in any and every situation, whether well fed or hungry, whether living in plenty or in want. I can do everything through him who gives me strength.

PHILIPPIANS 4:12–13

Remember the LORD your God, for it is he who gives you the ability to produce wealth, and so confirms his covenant, which he swore to your forefathers, as it is today.

DEUTERONOMY 8:18

There's no getting around it: people are motivated by rewards. God certainly understands this. Many people see God as a cosmic Scrooge who enjoys making people squirm and reluctantly hands out rewards for good behavior. But the Bible shows God as being quite the opposite. God is the lover of our souls—he delights in rewarding us with his joy!

Have you become enmeshed in a universe of "stuff," trying to be more, know more, make more? What have you lost? What have you gained? All it takes to be truly successful is to give yourself to Jesus.

Jesus said, "Store up for yourselves treasures in heaven, where moth and rust do not destroy, and where thieves do not break in and steal. For where your treasure is, there your heart will be also."

MATTHEW 6:20–21

Whoever trusts in his riches will fall,
but the righteous will thrive like a green leaf.

PROVERBS 11:28

"Bring the whole tithe into the storehouse, that there may be food in my house. Test me in this," says the LORD Almighty, "and see if I will not throw open the floodgates of heaven and pour out so much blessing that you will not have room enough for it."

MALACHI 3:10

Jesus said, "It is more blessed to give than to receive."

ACTS 20:35

We are told every day that success means having more—more money, more stuff, more power, more, more, more! But Jesus turned this idea upside down—he said less is more, and giving is better than having.

Jesus sat down opposite the place where the offerings were put and watched the crowd putting their money into the temple treasury. Many rich people threw in large amounts. But a poor widow came and put in two very small copper coins, worth only a fraction of a penny. Calling his disciples to him, Jesus said, "I tell you the truth, this poor widow has put more into the treasury than all the others. They all gave out of their wealth; but she, out of her poverty, put in everything—all she had to live on."

MARK 12:41–44

The world says, "The more you take, the more you have." Christ says, "The more you give, the more you are."

FREDERICK BUECHNER

The Need for
Self-Discipline

SELF-DISCIPLINE MAY BE *defined as that quality that allows a person to do what needs to be done when he or she doesn't feel like doing it. The apostle Paul understood the importance of discipline.*

We're to be like runners. During a race, runners don't stagger from one lane to another. They rivet their attention on the finish line and run a disciplined race toward it.

If you want to be like a winning runner, identify the habits you need to build into your life you can lead with diligence—habits such as physical fitness; balance between work, school, and home; financial and personal accountability; and regular conversation with God.

Strap on your shoes and get going! Discipline will give you the momentum you need to not only move forward, but also to run your earthly race with strength and purpose.

God did not
give us a spirit
of timidity, but
a spirit of power,
of love, and of
self-discipline.

2 TIMOTHY 1:7

*God disciplines us for our good, that we
may share in his holiness. No discipline
seems pleasant at the time, but painful.
Later on, however, it produces a harvest
of righteousness and peace for those
who have been trained by it.*

HEBREWS 12:10–11

*TRAIN YOURSELF TO BE
GODLY. FOR PHYSICAL
TRAINING IS OF SOME VALUE,
BUT GODLINESS HAS VALUE
FOR ALL THINGS, HOLDING
PROMISE FOR BOTH THE
PRESENT LIFE AND THE
LIFE TO COME.*

1 TIMOTHY 4:7–8

Blessed is the man you
discipline, O LORD,
the man you teach
from your law.

PSALM 94:12

My dear brothers, stand firm. Let nothing move you. Always give yourselves fully to the work of the Lord, because you know that your labor in the Lord is not in vain.

1 CORINTHIANS 15:58

I think the one benefit that a Christian has over a non-Christian is you can have self-discipline. You are not a slave to the flesh but you can be a slave to righteousness and have control. You can say no to drugs. You can say no to premarital sex. You don't have anything that latches hold to you and controls you that a non-believer would. It is so much easier to be disciplined and work. I think the difference between a lot of people and myself is that I worked like it depended on me, and prayed like it depended on God.

DAVID WOOD, FORMER NBA PLAYER

You have to get up each morning with a clear goal in mind saying to yourself, "Today, I'm going to do my best in every area. I'm not going to take the easy way; I'm going to give 100 percent."

TOM LANDRY,
FORMER COACH OF THE DALLAS COWBOYS

*The highway of the
upright avoids evil;
he who guards his
way guards his life.*

PROVERBS 16:17

Jesus prayed,

"Lead us not into

temptation,

but deliver us from

the evil one."

MATTHEW 6:13

*Because Jesus himself suffered when
he was tempted, he is able to help
those who are being tempted.*

HEBREWS 2:18

*The ability to say No! to temptation is not
some mystical power that belongs to a precious, select few. It belongs to you! Self-control can be evidenced in your life in very
practical ways. It means passing up the joint
or the bottle that is offered to you at a party.
It means walking a block out of your way to
avoid a magazine rack that tempts you. It
means not saying something you have every
right to say. And it means waging hand-to-
hand combat with the greatest temptations life
has to offer, not because you want to appear
righteous, but because God's best for your life
is better than anything in this world.*

S. RICKLY CHRISTIAN

The mind controlled by the
Spirit is life and peace.

ROMANS 8:6

Since ... you have been raised with Christ, set
your hearts on things above, where Christ is
seated at the right hand of God. Set your
minds on things above, not on earthly things.
For you died, and your life is now hidden
with Christ in God. When Christ, who is your
life, appears, then you also will appear with
him in glory.

COLOSSIANS 3:1–4

He who walks righteously
  and speaks what is right, ...
  and shuts his eyes against contemplating evil—
this is the man who will dwell on the heights,
  whose refuge will be the mountain fortress.
His bread will be supplied,
  and water will not fail him.

ISAIAH 33:15–16

The grace of God that brings salvation has appeared to all men. It teaches us to say "No" to ungodliness and worldly passions, and to live self-controlled, upright and godly lives in this present age, while we wait for the blessed hope—the glorious appearing of our great God and Savior, Jesus Christ.

TITUS 2:11–13

This is my prayer: that your love may abound more and more in knowledge and depth of insight, so that you may be able to discern what is best and may be pure and blameless until the day of Christ, filled with the fruit of righteousness that comes through Jesus Christ— to the glory and praise of God.

PHILIPPIANS 1:9–11

The fruit of righteousness will be peace;
the effect of righteousness will be
quietness and confidence forever.

ISAIAH 32:17

Setting Priorities

TAKE A FEW MINUTES *daily to ponder what is worthwhile about living. Stop whirling about like a pinwheel long enough to come to a rest and consider your next action. Just what is it you want to do? What do you need to do for the sake of your soul?*

LUCI SWINDOLL

We make it our goal
to please the Lord.

2 CORINTHIANS 5:9

Jesus said, "Do not worry, saying, 'What shall we eat?' or 'What shall we drink?' or 'What shall we wear?' ... Seek first God's kingdom and his righteousness, and all these things will be given to you as well."

MATTHEW 6:31, 33

Do what is right and good in the LORD's sight, so that it may go well with you.

DEUTERONOMY 6:18

Whatever you do, work at it with all your heart, as working for the Lord, not for men, since you know that you will receive an inheritance from the Lord as a reward. It is the Lord Christ you are serving.

COLOSSIANS 3:23–24

IMITATE THOSE WHO THROUGH FAITH AND PATIENCE INHERIT WHAT HAS BEEN PROMISED.

HEBREWS 6:12

I consider my life worth nothing to me, if only I may finish the race and complete the task the Lord Jesus has given me— the task of testifying to the gospel of God's grace.

ACTS 20:24

Jesus said, "Be faithful ... and I will give you the crown of life."

REVELATION 2:10

I've stumbled many times along the way and allowed my priorities to get out of line, but God has repeatedly shown me that I am to put nothing ahead of him in my life—not my wife, not my kids, not my ministry, and not my career. The more I'm able to put God first in all areas of my life, the more he's blessed me in them. When God is your top priority, that doesn't mean that you do it to the exclusion of the other areas of your life. When God is first in your life, those other areas take on a new, added importance simply because your heavenly Father is so interested in what you are doing. He wants to bless those other areas of your life simply because you glorify him when you succeed.

BRYCE PAUP,
FORMER PLAYER WITH THE BUFFALO BILLS

Does the LORD delight
in burnt offerings and
sacrifices as much as in
obeying the voice of the
LORD? To obey is better
than sacrifice.

1 SAMUEL 15:22

No matter what you do, just put God first. Be strongly committed to him, because without him we are nothing. And I don't want Jesus to think that what he did on the cross was in vain for me. I want to continue to do all that I can while I'm on this journey.

God sent his best gift in Jesus, so whenever you're in the classroom or whenever you're participating in sports or whatever it is, do it to the best of your ability.

AVERY JOHNSON, NBA PLAYER

*Whatever was to my profit I now
consider loss for the sake of Christ.
What is more, I consider everything
a loss compared to the surpassing
greatness of knowing Christ Jesus
my Lord, for whose sake I have lost
all things. I consider them rubbish,
that I may gain Christ and be found
in him, not having a righteousness
of my own that comes from the law,
but that which is through faith in
Christ—the righteousness that comes
from God and is by faith.*

PHILIPPIANS 3:7–9

*Because your love is better than life, Lord,
    my lips will glorify you.
I will praise you as long as I live,
    and in your name I will lift up my hands.*

PSALM 63:3–4

One of the teachers of the law came and heard them debating. Noticing that Jesus had given them a good answer, he asked him, "Of all the commandments, which is the most important?"

"The most important one," answered Jesus, "is this: 'Hear, O Israel, the Lord our God, the Lord is one. Love the Lord your God with all your heart and with all your soul and with all your mind and with all your strength.' The second is this: 'Love your neighbor as yourself.' There is no commandment greater than these."

MARK 12:28–31

Seek God's Guidance

GOD KNOWS OUR APTITUDES
and abilities better than we do ourselves.
He wants us to move toward the fulfillment
of our potential. But we cannot do this with-
out personal commitment to making Christ
first in our lives. Seek his guidance.

God said, "I guide you in the way of wisdom
and lead you along straight paths.
When you walk, your steps will not be hampered;
when you run, you will not stumble."

PROVERBS 4:11–12

It's comforting to know that God
guides you through life, no
matter what. He is always
leading you as you live for him.

The LORD gives wisdom,
and from his mouth
come knowledge and
understanding.

PROVERBS 2:6

> YOU WILL CALL, AND
> THE LORD WILL ANSWER;
> YOU WILL CRY FOR HELP,
> AND HE WILL SAY: HERE AM I.
>
> ISAIAH 58:9

Teach me knowledge and
good judgment, O LORD,
for I believe in your commands.

PSALM 119:66

Guide me in your truth
and teach me,
for you are
God my Savior,
and my hope is
in you all day long.

PSALM 25:5

Teach me to do your will, for you are my God;
may your good Spirit lead me on level ground.

PSALM 143:10

Hold onto instruction, do not let it go;
guard it well, for it is your life.

PROVERBS 4:13

He who scorns instruction will pay for it,
but he who respects a command is
rewarded.

PROVERBS 13:13

Search me, O God, and know my heart;
test me and know my anxious thoughts.
See if there is any offensive way in me,
and lead me in the way everlasting.

PSALM 139:23–24

Teach me, and I
will be quiet;
show me where I
have been wrong,
Lord.

JOB 6:24

Since you are my rock

and my fortress, LORD,

for the sake of your

name lead and guide me.

PSALM 31:3

Send forth your light and your truth, O God,
let them guide me;
let them bring me to your holy mountain,
to the place where you dwell.

PSALM 43:3

This God is our God for ever and ever;
he will be our guide even to the end.

PSALM 48:14

When I called, you answered me, LORD;
you made me bold and stouthearted.

PSALM 138:3

I was facing one of those momentous decision-making times. Having just finished my undergraduate degree, I needed to decide my next course of action. The number of options was staggering. Should I pursue graduate studies, or possibly get further spiritual and ministry training? Should I follow the "guy of my heart" and get married? Should I go overseas on a short-term missions project? Should I try to find a job? I felt that whatever choice I made would radically affect the rest of my life. I didn't know what to do.

Hoping to make the process easier, I tried to involve God. I prayed and read my Bible, but I still felt paralyzed with fear. As I tried to fig-ure out why, I realized that in my heart I really didn't trust God to answer me. I'd always pictured him as a kind of "Big Brother," watching over me not with eyes of love but eyes of judgment, waiting for me to make mistakes or choose the wrong path.

Then I came across Isaiah 30:21: "Whether you turn to the right or to the left, your ears will hear a voice behind you, saying, 'This is the way; walk in it.'" I was amazed. God is not watching me from far away, waiting for me to mess up. No, he is right here with me as I make decisions. He is so concerned for me that he will correct me if I take a wrong turn or get off the path. But I have to know his Word, listen for his voice, and have a heart to obey it— no matter what!

TINA LARSON

Meaningful Work

IT'S IMPORTANT TO KNOW *how to identify and cultivate a personal vision of your future work for the Lord. God will give you a vision of himself, and of the work "he is doing to this very day" (John 5:17).*

Through his Word he will show you what he is like and will give you insight into your spiritual destiny. As you seek him through his Word and through prayer, ask him to show you himself. Ask him to give you a clear image of the work he has called you to join him in accomplishing.

My heart took delight in all my work,
and this was the reward for all my labor.

ECCLESIASTES 2:10

May the favor of the LORD our God rest upon us;
establish the work of our hands for us—
yes, establish the work of our hands.

PSALM 90:17

Whatever your hand finds to do,
do it with all your might.

ECCLESIASTES 9:10

> WHATEVER YOU DO,
> WHETHER IN WORD OR DEED,
> DO IT ALL IN THE NAME
> OF THE LORD JESUS,
> GIVING THANKS TO
> GOD THE FATHER
> THROUGH HIM.
>
> COLOSSIANS 3:17

Jesus said, "My Father is
always at his work to this
very day, and I, too, am working."

JOHN 5:17

We are God's fellow workers;
you are God's field, God's building.

1 CORINTHIANS 3:9

We live in a materialistic culture where, all too often, a person's worth is measured by the size of his or her house, car or bank account. In this day of unparalleled opportunity and overwhelming advertising, it is tempting to pour all of our efforts into acquiring things for ourselves rather than to channel our energies toward the Lord's work.

As we have come to expect, God promises to help his people carry out his commands. "Be strong all you people of the land," declares the LORD, "and work. For I am with you," declares the LORD Almighty (Haggai 2:4). God calls us to give back to him and to do his work. But don't worry, he promises that his Spirit will remain with us. Holding on to his promises, this is something you can do.

God is not unjust; he
will not forget your work
and the love you have
shown him as you have
helped his people and
continue to help them.

HEBREWS 6:10

How will the Lord use your life this year? This month? This day? Is there one thing you can do to make life better for someone else? Can you warm the home of an elderly friend? Knock on the door of a lonely single mom? Invite a seven-year-old for lemonade? The possibilities are endless.

God expects us to use our brains and figure out what we can do to make a difference. Find out where he's working and join his crew.

BARBARA JOHNSON

May the God of peace, who through the blood of the eternal covenant brought back from the dead our Lord Jesus, that great Shepherd of the sheep, equip you with everything good for doing his will, and may he work in us what is pleasing to him, through Jesus Christ, to whom be glory for ever and ever.

HEBREWS 13:20–21

From the fruit of his lips a man is
filled with good things
as surely as the work
of his hands rewards him.

PROVERBS 12:14

Whatever you do, work at it with all your

heart, as working for the Lord, not for men,

since you know that you will receive an

inheritance from the Lord as a reward. It is the

Lord Christ you are serving.

COLOSSIANS 3:23–24

All hard work brings a profit.

PROVERBS 14:23

The desires of the

diligent are fully satisfied.

PROVERBS 13:4

Thank God—every morning when you get up—that you have something to do which must be done, whether you like it or not. Being forced to work, and forced to do your best, will breed in you a hundred virtues which those who do nothing will never know.

CHARLES KINGSLEY

Do you see a man skilled in his work?
He will serve before kings;
he will not serve before obscure men.

PROVERBS 22:29

When God gives any man wealth and possessions, and enables him to enjoy them, to accept his lot and be happy in his work—this is a gift of God.

ECCLESIASTES 5:19

The Need for
Lifelong Learning

AS A PERSON COMMITTED *to God, you should practice what is known as "double-loop" learning. When an issue or problem arises—in your life or in someone else's—analyze the first loop: the behavior. Then, study closely the second loop: the values and attitudes that drive behavior.*

By practicing "double-loop" learning, we can pull apart the confusing ways of this world and come to a deeper understanding of God's way.

Test me, O LORD, and try me,
*   examine my heart and my mind.*

PSALM 26:2

To the man who
pleases him, God
gives wisdom,
knowledge and
happiness.

ECCLESIASTES 2:26

This is my prayer: that your love may abound more and more in knowledge and depth of insight, so that you may be able to discern what is best and may be pure and blameless until the day of Christ.

PHILIPPIANS 1:9-10

A WISE MAN HAS
GREAT POWER,
AND A MAN OF
KNOWLEDGE INCREASES
STRENGTH.

PROVERBS 24:5

The heart of the discerning acquires knowledge; the ears of the wise seek it out.

PROVERBS 18:15

Wisdom—the accumulation of lifelong learning—seems to be in short supply. Some people are crafty and shrewd, others are well-informed and highly educated, but few manifest the quiet depth of wisdom.

Wisdom is the ability to use the best means at the best time to achieve the best ends. It is not merely a matter of information, skills, talents, or knowledge, but of skillful and practical application of the truth to multiple facets of life.

The underlying principle of wisdom is this: the person who refuses to act on what he or she knows, who refuses counsel, who ignores advice, will get in trouble. When he or she searches for some intelligent way out of the pit, there will be no wisdom left.

The next time you hear someone (or yourself!) saying, "I should have known better," or "How could I have been so stupid?" you will recognize "wisdom after the fact."

Wisdom —the
most valuable
accumulation
of learning
there is—calls
to us. Listen.

Get wisdom, get
*   understanding;*
*   do not forget my words*
*   or swerve from them.*
Do not forsake wisdom,
*   and she will protect you;*
*   love her, and she will*
*   watch over you.*
Wisdom is supreme; there-
*   fore get wisdom.*

PROVERBS 4:5–7

To God belong wisdom and power;
*   counsel and understanding are his.*

JOB 12:13

Surely you desire truth in the inner parts, O LORD;
*   you teach me wisdom in the inmost place.*

PSALM 51:6

*Blessed are those who have learned
to acclaim you,
who walk in the light of your
presence, O LORD.*

PSALM 89:15

*Instruct a wise man and he will be wiser still;
teach a righteous man and he will add to
his learning.
The fear of the LORD is the beginning of wisdom,
and knowledge of the Holy One is
understanding.*

PROVERBS 9:9–10

*Jesus said, "Take my yoke upon you and learn
from me, for I am gentle and humble in heart,
and you will find rest for your souls. For my
yoke is easy and my burden is light."*

MATTHEW 11:29–30

*All Scripture is God-breathed and is useful for
teaching, rebuking, correcting and training in
righteousness, so that the man of God may be
thoroughly equipped for every good work.*

2 TIMOTHY 3:16–17

The word wisdom brings up pictures of gray-haired old men muttering obscure philosophic maxims. But that is almost the opposite of what the biblical book of Proverbs means by the word. Wisdom is above all practical and down-to-earth. Young people as well as old can and should have it. Wisdom teaches you how to live. It combines understanding with discipline— the kind of discipline an athlete needs in training. It also adds a healthy dose of good common sense—except that common sense isn't, and never has been, common.

How do you become a wise person? You must first begin to listen. Wisdom is freely available to those who will stop talking and start paying attention—to God and his Word, to parents, to wise counselors. Anybody can become wise, Proverbs says. Wisdom is not reserved for the brainy elite. But becoming wise requires self-discipline to study and humbly seek wisdom at every opportunity.

THE NIV STUDENT BIBLE

Embracing Change

IN MANY ASPECTS OF LIFE *today, people are asked to "Eat change ... drink change ... sleep change"... or be prepared to have a 'change' in their status!*

The only certainty is that things will change.

It's a rapidly changing world we live in; be prepared to take it head-on with our Lord at your side! (His love is the one thing that never changes!)

Jesus Christ is the same
yesterday and
today and forever.

HEBREWS 13:8

The Father of the heavenly lights ... does not change like shifting shadows.

JAMES 1:17

I the LORD
do not change.

MALACHI 3:6

God's dominion is an everlasting dominion
that will not pass away, and his kingdom is
one that will never be destroyed.

DANIEL 7:14

*Live for today but hold your hands open
to tomorrow. Anticipate the future and its
changes with joy. There is a seed of God's
love in every event, every circumstance,
every unpleasant situation in which you
may find yourself. Don't get stuck in a rut
or hung up on an outdated blessing.
You serve a God of change!*

BARBARA JOHNSON

*AND WHILE GOD NEVER
CHANGES WHO HE IS,
WE CAN BE THANKFUL
THAT HE DOES CHANGE
US—FOR THE BETTER!*

*If anyone is in Christ, he is a new creation;
the old has gone, the new has come!*

2 CORINTHIANS 5:17

*"Forget the former things;
  do not dwell on the past.
See, I am doing a new thing!
  Now it springs up; do you not perceive it?
I am making a way in the desert
  and streams in the wasteland," says the LORD.*

ISAIAH 43:18–19

*Listen, I tell you a mystery: We will not all
sleep, but we will all be changed—in a
flash, in the twinkling of an eye, at the last
trumpet. For the trumpet will sound, the
dead will be raised imperishable, and we
will be changed. For the perishable must
clothe itself with the imperishable, and the
mortal with immortality.*

1 CORINTHIANS 15:51–53

Dear friends, now we are
children of God, and
what we will be has not
yet been made known.
But we know that when
he appears, we shall be
like him, for we shall see
him as he is.

1 JOHN 3:2

We, who with unveiled faces all reflect the

Lord's glory, are being transformed into his

likeness with ever-increasing glory, which

comes from the Lord, who is the Spirit.

2 CORINTHIANS 3:18

"Behold, I will create
new heavens and a new earth.
The former things will not be remembered,
nor will they come to mind.
But be glad and rejoice forever
in what I will create," says the LORD.

ISAIAH 65:17–18

*Life boasts very few things that are
absolutely dependable, but change is
one of them, and it is the one we seem
to fear most.*

*The moon and the ocean both provide
exquisite models of the rhythm of life—
consistent in their waxing and waning,
advance and retreat, ebb and flow. But in our
brief earth journey, most of us just haven't
been quite able to get the hang of it. We dread
the ebbing, fearing the flow will never return.
We want it to be all flow ...
We demand permanency as security
against loss when, in reality, the only way
to keep what we have is to allow it freedom to
change and grow.*

*In God's infinite understanding of the human
condition, he reaches out to assuage the dread
and fear of change: "Trust me," he says, "I
will never leave you nor forsake you."*

JOY MACKENZIE

One day, God will make the ultimate change to all of creation, and that change will bring us his perfection!

Then I saw a new heaven and a new earth, for the first heaven and the first earth had passed away, and there was no longer any sea. I saw the Holy City, the new Jerusalem, coming down out of heaven from God, prepared as a bride beautifully dressed for her husband. And I heard a loud voice from the throne saying, "Now the dwelling of God is with men, and he will live with them. They will be his people, and God himself will be with them and be their God. He will wipe every tear from their eyes. There will be no more death or mourning or crying or pain, for the old order of things has passed away." He who was seated on the throne said, "I am making everything new!"

REVELATION 21:1–5

Making the Most
of Our Time

We spend time, save time, waste time, lose time, take time, make time, trade time for money, do things in "real time," and just generally wish for more time.

We know, at a fairly early age, that time passes. We are not immortal. We have a finite amount of time in this life.

But rather than making the most of our time, many of us worry about it! We buy expensive calendars, personal digital organizers, and as many time-saving gadgets and conveniences as we can afford! We try hard not to waste time, but we don't think enough about how to spend it.

Each of us has been allotted a finite number of days. Are we spending them wandering aimlessly, with no goal, no purpose in sight? Or are we using them to gain a heart of wisdom?

Teach us to number our days aright,
*   that we may gain a heart of wisdom.*

PSALM 90:12

Show me, O LORD, my life's end and the num-
ber of my days;
  let me know how fleeting is my life.
You have made my days
  a mere handbreadth;
  the span of my years is as nothing before
  you.
Each man's life is but a breath.
  Man is a mere phantom as he goes to and fro:
He bustles about, but only in vain;
  he heaps up wealth, not knowing who will
  get it.
But now, LORD, what do I look for?
  My hope is in you.

PSALM 39:4–7

Make the most of every opportunity. Let your conversation be always full of grace, seasoned with salt, so that you may know how to answer everyone.

COLOSSIANS 4:5–6

You do not even know

what will happen tomorrow.

What is your life? You are

but a mist that appears

for a little while and

then vanishes. ... You ought

to say, "If it is the Lord's

will, we will live and

do this or that."

JAMES 4:14–15

LIFE ISN'T A DESTINATION BUT A JOURNEY,

and so we all encounter unexpected curves,

turning points, mountaintops, and valleys. We

discover the best in ourselves as each event

occurs and shapes us into who we are. The

trip can be a long one, but we can support

each other on the way by loving, caring, and

softening the blows.

God is the one who knows our future and the

paths we will take during our journey. He

fine-tunes us so those who are watching can

admire his handiwork in us. And we can be

assured that, because of him, life will always

offer us beautiful vistas.

BARBARA JOHNSON

*As we have opportunity,
let us do good to all people,
especially to those who
belong to the family
of believers.*

GALATIANS 6:10

*My salvation and my honor depend on God;
he is my mighty rock, my refuge.
Trust in him at all times, O people;
pour out your hearts to him,
for God is our refuge.*

PSALM 62:7–8

Be very careful ... how you
live—not as unwise but
as wise, making the most
of every opportunity.

EPHESIANS 5:15–16

Place a high value on your time, be more careful of not losing it than you would of losing your money. Do not let anything rob you of your precious time.... Be more careful to escape that person, action or course of life that would rob you of your time than you would be to escape thieves and robbers.

RICHARD BAXTER

Stewardship: Using What We Have Been Given

STEWARDSHIP IS A BIG *word used to describe a fairly simple concept: God has made an investment in each of us. He has blessed us with resources, talents, and gifts. If we use them well, for the glorification of God and for the good of others, we are exhibiting good stewardship. If we use them unwisely, there will be no "return" in God's final accounting.*

We should live in a way to make God a "smart investor" by multiplying the resources he has placed in our trust.

Jesus said, "Give, and it will be given to you. A good measure, pressed down, shaken together and running over, will be poured into your lap. For with the measure you use, it will be measured to you."

LUKE 6:38

Turn my heart toward your statutes, Lord, and not toward selfish gain.

PSALM 119:36

Every good and perfect gift is from above.

JAMES 1:17

WE ARE GOD'S WORKMANSHIP,
CREATED IN CHRIST JESUS TO
DO GOOD WORKS, WHICH
GOD PREPARED IN ADVANCE
FOR US TO DO.

EPHESIANS 2:10

Rejoice in all the good things
the LORD your God has
given to you.

DEUTERONOMY 26:11

Fan into flame the gift of God,
which is in you through the
laying on of my hands.
For God did not give us
a spirit of timidity, but a
spirit of power, of love
and of self-discipline.

2 TIMOTHY 1:6–7

Remember this: Whoever sows
sparingly will also reap sparingly,
and whoever sows generously will also
reap generously. Each man should give
what he has decided in his heart to give,
not reluctantly or under compulsion, for
God loves a cheerful giver. And God is able
to make all grace abound to you, so that in
all things at all times, having all that you
need, you will abound in every good work.

2 CORINTHIANS 9:6–8

We have different gifts, according to
the grace given us. If a man's gift is
prophesying, let him use it in proportion to
his faith. If it is serving, let him serve;
if it is teaching, let him teach; if it is
encouraging, let him encourage; if it is
contributing to the needs of others, let him
give generously; if it is leadership, let him
govern diligently; if it is showing mercy,
let him do it cheerfully.

ROMANS 12:6–8

Today when we speak of
a "talented" musician or
athlete, we are actually
harking back to the
parable of the talents
recorded in Matthew 25.

*A talent in Jesus' time was a valuable sum
of money worth about two years' wages.
Because of this parable, the word has
acquired a different meaning. Each person
in the kingdom of heaven is given a
certain number of gifts and opportunities
(talents) to serve God. We can either
waste those opportunities or invest
them in a way that furthers the kingdom.*

Jesus said, "After a long time the master of
those servants returned and settled accounts
with them. The man who had received
the five talents brought the other five.
'Master,' he said, 'you entrusted me with
five talents. See, I have gained five more.'

"His master replied, 'Well done, good
and faithful servant! You have been
faithful with a few things; I will put
you in charge of many things.
Come and share your
master's happiness!'"

MATTHEW 25:19–21

All the blessings
we enjoy are Divine
deposits, committed to
our trust on this
condition, that they
should be dispensed
for the benefit of
our neighbors.

JOHN CALVIN

You will be made rich in every way so that

you can be generous on every occasion, and

through us your generosity will result in

thanksgiving to God. This service that you

perform is not only supplying the needs of

God's people but is also overflowing in many

expressions of thanks to God.

2 CORINTHIANS 9:11-12

Jesus said, "The King will say to those on his right, 'Come, you who are blessed by my Father; take your inheritance, the kingdom prepared for you since the creation of the world. For I was hungry and you gave me something to eat, I was thirsty and you gave me something to drink, I was a stranger and you invited me in, I needed clothes and you clothed me, I was sick and you looked after me, I was in prison and you came to visit me.'"

"Then the righteous will answer him, 'Lord, when did we see you hungry and feed you, or thirsty and give you something to drink? When did we see you a stranger and invite you in, or needing clothes and clothe you? When did we see you sick or in prison and go to visit you?'"

"The King will reply, 'I tell you the truth, whatever you did for one of the least of these brothers of mine, you did for me.'"

MATTHEW 25:34–40

Setting an Example

AS A GRADUATE—A PERSON *who has had the privilege of a good education —you are in a unique position to help others develop their own skills and knowledge and to reach their full potential. You can help them become all that God created them to be.*

Set an example. Lead. Listen for God's guidance, then embody it in words and actions so that others may see, hear, and learn from your example.

Don't let anyone look down on you because you are young, but set an example for the believers in speech, in life, in love, in faith, and in purity.

1 TIMOTHY 4:12

Christ suffered for you, leaving you an example, that you should follow in his steps.

1 PETER 2:21

Jesus said, "Whoever wants to become
great among you must be your servant,
and whoever wants to be first must be
slave of all. For even the Son of Man
did not come to be served, but to serve,
and to give his life as a ransom for many."

MARK 10:43–45

BE IMITATORS OF GOD,
THEREFORE, AS DEARLY
LOVED CHILDREN AND
LIVE A LIFE OF LOVE,
JUST AS CHRIST LOVED
US AND GAVE HIMSELF
UP FOR US AS A
FRAGRANT OFFERING
AND SACRIFICE TO GOD.

EPHESIANS 5:1–2

*Being a Christian means being concerned
about the disparity between how we live
and how we look, between what we do and
what we say. It helps to know God doesn't
just care what we do on Sundays; he cares
how we live and act the other six days as
well. He cares that our Christianity is
evidenced in every part of our lives: the
mental, social, physical ... as well as
the spiritual.*

S. RICKLY CHRISTIAN

Who is wise and understanding
among you? Let him show
it by his good life, by deeds
done in the humility that
comes from wisdom.

JAMES 3:13

Jesus said,
"Let your light
shine before
men, that they
may see your
good deeds
and praise
your Father
in heaven."

MATTHEW 5:16

When Jesus had finished washing [his disciples'] feet, he put on his clothes and returned to his place. "Do you understand what I have done for you?" he asked them. "You call me 'Teacher' and 'Lord,' and rightly so, for that is what I am. Now that I, your Lord and Teacher, have washed your feet, you also should wash one another's feet. I have set you an example that you should do as I have done for you."

JOHN 13:12–15

We are therefore Christ's ambassadors, as though God were making his appeal through us. We implore you on Christ's behalf: Be reconciled to God. God made him who had no sin to be sin for us, so that in him we might become the righteousness of God. As God's fellow workers we urge you not to receive God's grace in vain.

2 CORINTHIANS 5:20–6:1

I will praise you,
O Lord, with all
my heart;
I will tell of all
your wonders.

PSALM 9:1

Restore to me the joy of your salvation, Lord,
  and grant me a willing spirit, to sustain me.
Then I will teach transgressors your ways, and
  sinners will turn back to you

PSALM 51:12–13

My mouth will tell of your righteousness,
  of your salvation all day long, though I
  know not its measure.
I will come and proclaim your mighty acts, O
  Sovereign Lord!
  I will proclaim your righteousness, yours
  alone.

PSALM 71:15–16

May the God of peace, who through the blood
of the eternal covenant brought back from the
dead our Lord Jesus, that great Shepherd of
the sheep, equip you with everything good for
doing his will, and may he work in us what is
pleasing to him, through Jesus Christ, to
whom be glory for ever and ever. Amen.

HEBREWS 13:20–21

Reviewing old yearbooks is sort of like entering a time warp. You aren't the same person you were back then. Times have changed, and you have, too.

Take some time and dig out your yearbooks. Read what people wrote about you. What adjectives surface most frequently in their descriptions of you? Nice? Bodacious? Crazy? Party animal? Quiet? Brainy? Driven? Funny?

As you flip through the pages, keep track of the adjectives that surface most frequently. Are any of them like those used to describe Christians in the Bible: compassionate, kind, humble, forgiving, loving, thankful?

Christ said each of us is to be a light to our own corner of the world. You should be the bright spot in people's lives. If you truly are, you'll read about it in your yearbooks.

S. RICKLY CHRISTIAN

Communication
Is the Key

BECAUSE WE HAVE BEEN *created in the likeness of God, we are personal, relational, communicating beings. The issue is not whether we will communicate, but how effective and appropriate our communication will be.*

We all spend vast amounts of time talking! We chat, we persuade, we inform, we dispute, we joke, we shout, and we talk, talk, talk!

But we don't spend much time learning how to listen. Listening, which leads to understanding, is the most important communication skill we can develop.

Closely tied to the skill of listening is the ability to express oneself in a nonabrasive and affirming manner.

Our speech can be a blessing—or an injury— to others.

We must think before we speak, and by so doing we select words that nurture, not destroy.

Listening and speaking skillfully—and joyfully—creates two-way communication. And communication in which both parties are equally engaged creates caring, trust, and confidence.

A word aptly spoken
is like apples of gold in settings of silver.

PROVERBS 25:11

The Sovereign Lord has given me an instructed
tongue,
to know the word that sustains the weary.
He wakens me morning by morning,
wakens my ear to listen like one being
taught.

ISAIAH 50:4

A MAN FINDS JOY IN GIVING
AN APT REPLY—AND
HOW GOOD IS A
TIMELY WORD!

PROVERBS 15:23

Do not let unwholesome talk
come out of your mouths,
but only what is helpful for
building others up according
to their needs, that it may
benefit those who listen.

EPHESIANS 4:29

Let your conversation be always full of grace, seasoned with salt, so that you may know how to answer everyone.

COLOSSIANS 4:6

An honest answer
is like a kiss on the lips.

PROVERBS 24:26

From the fruit of his lips a man is filled
with good things
as surely as the work of his hands
rewards him.

PROVERBS 12:14

Speak, LORD, for your
servant is listening.

1 SAMUEL 3:9

May the words of
*   my mouth and the*
*   meditation of my*
*   heart be pleasing in*
*   your sight,*
*   O Lord, my Rock and*
*   my Redeemer.*

PSALM 19:14

Gold there is, and rubies in abundance,
*   but lips that speak knowledge are a rare*
*   jewel.*

PROVERBS 20:15

The tongue that brings
healing is a tree of life.

PROVERBS 15:4

Come and listen, all you who fear God;
*   let me tell you what he has done for me.*

PSALM 66:16

*Everyone should be quick
to listen, slow to speak.*

JAMES 1:19

Speaking the truth in love,
we will in all things grow
up into him who is the Head,
that is, Christ.

EPHESIANS 4:15

*Speak to one another with psalms,
hymns and spiritual songs. Sing
and make music in your heart
to the LORD, always giving thanks
to God the Father for everything,
in the name of our Lord Jesus Christ.*

EPHESIANS 5:19–20

If anyone speaks,
he should do it as
one speaking the
very words of God.

1 PETER 4:11

Wisdom is knowing when to speak your mind and when to mind your speech.

AUTHOR UNKNOWN

Whatever you do, whether
in word or deed, do it all
in the name of the Lord
Jesus, giving thanks to
God the Father through him.

COLOSSIANS 3:17

*Jesus said, "The good man brings good
things out of the good stored
up in his heart. ... For out of
the overflow of his heart
his mouth speaks."*

LUKE 6:45

*Kind words can be short and easy to speak but
their echoes are truly endless.*

MOTHER TERESA

Plug into the
Power of Prayer

SWEATING. AGONIZING. GRUNTING.
*Groaning. Straining. Thinking. Strategizing.
Planning. Attacking. Using strength. Using
balance. Using leverage. How often do those
terms, which can easily describe a wrestling
match, describe our conversations with God?
How often do we get that serious with God
when we talk with him?*

*Try wrestling in prayer the next time you
go before the Lord. See what kind of energy
and effort it takes to petition God for your
requests. You might even work up some
holy sweat!*

THE SPORTS DEVOTIONAL BIBLE

Devote yourselves
to prayer, being
watchful and
thankful.

COLOSSIANS 4:2

The prayer of a righteous man is
powerful and effective.

JAMES 5:16

Jesus said, "When you pray, go into your
room, close the door and pray to your Father,
who is unseen. Then your Father, who sees
what is done in secret, will reward you."

MATTHEW 6:6

JESUS SAID, "IF YOU BELIEVE,
YOU WILL RECEIVE WHATEVER
YOU ASK FOR IN PRAYER."

MATTHEW 21:22

How gracious God will be
when you cry for help!
As soon as he hears,
he will answer you.

ISAIAH 30:19

The eyes of the LORD are on the righteous,
and his ears are attentive to their prayer.

1 PETER 3:12

"You will call upon me and come and pray to me, and I will listen to you. You will seek me and find me when you seek me with all your heart," says the LORD.

JEREMIAH 29:12–13

Pray in the Spirit on all occasions with all kinds of prayers and requests. With this in mind be alert and always keep on praying for all the saints.

EPHESIANS 6:18

Jesus said, "Ask and it will be given to you; seek and you will find; knock and the door will be opened to you. For everyone who asks, receives; he who seeks finds; and to him who knocks, the door will be opened."

MATTHEW 7:7–8

We do not know what to pray for, but the Spirit himself intercedes for us with groans that words cannot express.

ROMANS 8:26

Come near to God and

he will come near to you.

JAMES 4:8

Given the emphasis the Bible puts on prayer, I believe God longs just to hear our voices. And not just when we're in trouble —sometimes just to chat.

Yet people make prayer seem so formal. They prescribe everything from stance (on your knees) to timing (preferably before sunrise). Others use a special language (Thy, Thou, Thine), while some think you can't talk to God directly—you must first go through an "operator" (such as a priest). There's only one problem with all this formality:

Christ was often very informal in the way he prayed.

In the Garden of Gethsemane, shortly before his trial and crucifixion, Jesus grew deeply distressed. The Bible says he fell to the ground and prayed, "Abba, Father ..." He addressed God not just as Father, but as Abba, meaning Daddy.

Remember —we are God's children. That means we have direct access to him, anytime. And we don't need to address him as "Sir" or "Almighty God." Daddy is good enough.

Our Father never tires of hearing his children's voices.

S. RICKLY CHRISTIAN

Next time you think you hear nothing in response to your prayers, don't assume God isn't listening. He may simply want you to rest in his shadow until he reveals his answer. When you hear a direct no, remind yourself there will always be a better yes. God is for you, and he will work out everything in conformity with the purpose of his will. Everything.

KATHY TROCCOLI

In the morning, O LORD, you hear my voice; in the morning I lay my requests before you and wait in expectation.

PSALM 5:3

Are you feeling long on need and short on resources? Let me encourage you to do what I do when I feel that way: go to the one who has promised to provide everything you need, in abundance. God may not give you the answer you had envisioned, but you can trust it to be the perfect provision. He has promised his fullness. No half remedies. No special deals.

LUCI SWINDOLL

No one has heard,
    no ear has perceived,
no eye has seen any God besides you,
    who acts on behalf of those who wait for him.

ISAIAH 64:4

God has surely listened
    and heard my voice in prayer.
Praise be to God,
    who has not rejected my prayer
    or withheld his love from me!

PSALM 66:19–20

IT'S APPROPRIATE THAT CHRIST *referred to the act of becoming a Christian as being "born again." In God's eyes you are a newborn infant—and he wants to train you his way. That training process is difficult. At times, very difficult. But God has not left you to blunder your way in darkness like some sadistic father who turns the light out on his wobble-kneed infant and then laughs when the kid smashes into a table.*

Rather, "God works in you to will and act according to his good purpose." That's to say he helps you in your Christian walk, and he's there to pick you up again if you fall. It's when you take his outstretched hand and follow him that walking feels like second nature. And it's then that you feel most able to not just walk, but to "run and not grow weary."

S. RICKLY CHRISTIAN

Jesus said, "God so loved the world that he gave his one and only Son, that whoever believes in him shall not perish but have eternal life."

138

JOHN 3:16

You have been born again, not of perishable seed, but of imperishable, through the living and enduring word of God.

1 PETER 1:23

Praise be to God and Father of our Lord Jesus Christ! In his great mercy he has given us new birth into a living hope through the resurrection of Jesus Christ from the dead, and into an inheritance that can never perish, spoil or fade—kept in heaven for you.

1 PETER 1:3–4

THE GIFT OF GOD IS
ETERNAL LIFE IN
CHRIST JESUS OUR LORD.

ROMANS 6:23

To all who received him, to those who believed in his name, he gave the right to become children of God—children born not of natural descent, nor of human decision or a husband's will, but born of God.

JOHN 1:12–13

You might wonder, what's the difference between a Christian and a non-Christian? "If anyone is in Christ," the apostle Paul wrote, "he is a new creation; the old has gone, the new has come."

In other words, when people become Christians, their insides are transformed. They aren't quite the same anymore. New life has begun!

S. RICKLY CHRISTIAN

Create in me a pure heart, O God,
and renew a steadfast spirit within me.

PSALM 51:10

*Do not conform any
longer to the pattern of
this world, but be trans-
formed by the renewing
of your mind. Then you
will be able to test and
approve what God's will
is—his good, pleasing
and perfect will.*

ROMANS 12:2

We do not lose heart. Though outwardly we
are wasting away, yet inwardly we are being
renewed day by day. For our light and
momentary troubles are achieving for us an
eternal glory that far outweighs them all. So
we fix our eyes not on what is seen, but on
what is unseen. For what is seen is temporary,
but what is unseen is eternal.

2 CORINTHIANS 4:16–18

*God saved us, not because
of righteous things we
had done, but because of
his mercy. He saved us through
the washing of rebirth and
renewal by the Holy Spirit,
whom he poured out on us
generously through Jesus
Christ our Savior.*

TITUS 3:5–6

Five years ago I came to believe in Christ's teaching, and my life suddenly changed; I ceased to desire what I had previously desired, and begin to desire what I formerly did not want. What had previously seemed to me good seemed evil, and what had seemed evil seemed good. It happened to me as it happens to a man who goes out on some business and on the way suddenly decides that the business is unnecessary and returns home. All that was on his right is not on his left, and all that was on his left is not now his right; his former wish to get as far as possible from home has changed into a wish to be as near as possible to it. The direction of my life and my desires became different, and good and evil changed places.

LEO TOLSTOY

Put on the new self, which is
being renewed in knowledge in
the image of its Creator.

COLOSSIANS 3:10

We were ... buried with Christ through bap-
tism into death in order that, just as Christ
was raised from the dead through the glory
of the Father, we too may live a new life.

ROMANS 6:4

You were taught, with regard to
your former way of life, to put
off your old self, which is being
corrupted by its deceitful desires;
to be made new in the attitude
of your minds; and to put on
the new self, created to be like God
in true righteousness and holiness.

EPHESIANS 4:22–24

"I will give you a new heart and
put a new spirit in you; I will remove
from you your heart of stone and give
*you a heart of flesh," says the L*ORD*.*

EZEKIEL 36:26

All Things in Time

IN OUR INCREASINGLY *fast-paced world, we've come to expect instant solutions to our personal pressures and daily trials. We don't want a timely struggle with our problems— we'd prefer to catapult over them. We want to smile and feel happy and say "Praise the Lord!" a lot.*

So we attend all kinds of Bible studies, victory rallies, youth camps, super Sunday seminars, and revival meetings to discover the spiritual key and that hidden verse that will help us combat "what's wrong" in our lives.

Yet, what's wrong is that we want answers NOW! And if our minister can't provide them, we'll hop to another church to get a spiritual fix that hopefully will numb the panic and pressure we feel about school, work, a personal relationship, our future, or our families.

The daily frustrations we want off our backs are the very things the Bible says we not only ought to endure, but endure joyfully.

The joy comes in knowing the difficulties we face help us grow spiritually. And so it is: God is at work in our lives, turning our biggest irritants into priceless gems. It's a timely process that can't be rushed.

S. RICKLY CHRISTIAN

*A patient man has
great understanding.*

PROVERBS 14:29

Better a patient
man than a warrior.

PROVERBS 16:32

> BE COMPLETELY HUMBLE
> AND GENTLE; BE PATIENT,
> BEARING WITH ONE
> ANOTHER IN LOVE.
>
> EPHESIANS 4:2

The end of a matter is better
than its beginning,
and patience is better
than pride.

ECCLESIASTES 7:8

Be joyful in hope, patient
in affliction, faithful in prayer.

ROMANS 12:12

Live every day to fulfill your personal

mission. God has a reason for whatever

season you are living through right now.

A season of loss or blessing? A season of

activity or hibernation? A season of

growth or incubation? You may think

you're on a detour, but God knows the

best way for you to reach your destination.

BARBARA JOHNSON

*Christ was sacrificed once to take away the
sins of many people; and he will appear a
second time, not to bear sin, but to bring
salvation to those who are waiting for him.*

HEBREWS 9:28

I waited patiently for the LORD; he turned to me and heard my cry.

PSALM 40:1

THERE IS A TIME FOR EVERYTHING, AND A SEASON FOR EVERY ACTIVITY UNDER HEAVEN:

a time to be born and a time to die,

a time to plant and a time to uproot,

a time to kill and a time to heal,

a time to tear down and a time to build,

a time to weep and a time to laugh,

a time to mourn and a time to dance,

a time to scatter stones and a time to gather them,

a time to embrace and a time to refrain,

a time to search and a time to give up,

a time to keep and a time to throw away,

a time to tear and a time to mend,

a time to be silent and a time to speak,

a time to love and a time to hate,

a time for war and a time for peace.

ECCLESIASTES 3:1–8

*Be patient ... until the Lord's
coming. See how the farmer
waits for the land to yield its
valuable crop and how patient
he is for the autumn and spring
rains. You, too, be patient
and stand firm, because
the Lord's coming is near.*

JAMES 5:7–8

*I wait for the LORD, my soul waits,
  and in his word I put my hope.
My soul waits for the Lord
  more than watchmen wait for the morning,
  more than watchmen wait for the morning.*

PSALM 130:5–6

*The Lord is not slow in keeping his promise,
as some understand slowness. He is patient
with you, not wanting anyone to perish, but
everyone to come to repentance.*

2 PETER 3:9

God has made everything
beautiful in its time.

ECCLESIASTES 3:11

*Waiting is God's school, where we learn
some of his most valuable lessons for us.*

AUTHOR UNKNOWN

*So often, our life seems as dull and flat as
the prairie. But when we invite God into
our lives we see extra richness and excite-
ment in even the flattest of fields. Things
that seemed dull and one-dimensional,
such as certain jobs or certain people, are
often blossoming and full of life—if we're
willing to look through God's eyes. God can
make the ordinary task of waiting into the
extraordinary experience of discovering.*

LEE STUART

*Jesus said, "The kingdom of heaven is
like a mustard seed, which a man took and
planted in his field. Though it is the
smallest of all your seeds, yet when it
grows, it is the largest of garden plants and
becomes a tree, so that the birds of the air
come and perch in its branches."*

MATTHEW 13:31–32

*In the morning, O LORD, you hear my voice;
in the morning I lay my requests before you
and wait in expectation.*

PSALM 5:3

Trust: God's "Got Your Back"

IN OUR DAY-TO-DAY LIVES, *we're much like misguided drivers on a busy freeway. We rely on our own limited perspective as we face our futures and the road ahead. But God views the world like a traffic controller, scoping the roadways that stretch from horizon to horizon. He sees the roads you roam—where you've been and where you're headed. He knows where the detours are.*

But God doesn't just watch—he directs. You're not just another somebody lost in the rush of life. You're a unique creation of his that he will lovingly guide along the route he feels is best for you, according to his broader perspective.

S. RICKLY CHRISTIAN

Those who know your name will trust in you, for you, LORD, have never forsaken those who seek you.

PSALM 9:10

Surely God is my salvation; I will trust and not be afraid.

ISAIAH 12:2

I am not ashamed because I know whom I have believed, and am convinced that God is able to guard what I have entrusted to him.

2 TIMOTHY 1:12

> *JESUS SAID, "DO NOT LET YOUR HEARTS BE TROUBLED. TRUST IN GOD; TRUST ALSO IN ME."*
>
> JOHN 14:1

"When you pass through the waters,
I will be with you;
and when you pass through the rivers,
they will not sweep over you.
When you walk through the fire,
you will not be burned;
the flames will not set you ablaze," says the LORD.

ISAIAH 43:2

There is no situation in this life that God will not miraculously lead us through—giving us a strength and peace that we know is beyond anything we could conjure up. Lean on him. Abandon yourself to his grace. God will give you strength when you need it.

As changes take place in my life, I continue to watch them truly work out for my good—if I can just wait on God to see me through. What makes all the difference is trust—the understanding that God has a much bigger plan than mine even if I don't understand it. I'm grateful, yet sorry, that I have had to learn so many lessons by hindsight.

Keep looking to God. Keep trusting in him. Know that he is always leading you to a higher place —let him. The road may look strange to you. You may feel lost, or far behind, or confused. But if you follow Jesus, it will be the right road, and in the end you will have peace. For peace is found only in the center of God's will.

KATHY TROCCOLI

The LORD's

unfailing love

surrounds the man

who trusts in him.

PSALM 32:10

The LORD delights in a man's way,
  he makes his steps firm;
though he stumble, he will not fall,
  for the LORD upholds him with his hand.

PSALM 37:23–24

"I will save you ... because you
trust in me," declares the LORD.

JEREMIAH 39:18

Over the years, God has been faithful to
his work, protecting me and providing
for me at every turn. I've never regretted
the decision to trust God.

RITZ SCHWEITZ

*Trust in the L*ORD *and do good;*
   dwell in the land and enjoy safe pasture.
*Delight yourself in the L*ORD
   and he will give you the desires of your heart.
*Commit your way to the L*ORD*;*
   trust in him and he will do this:
He will make your righteousness shine like the dawn,
   the justice of your cause like the noonday sun.

PSALM 37:3–6

Trust God for great things; with your five
loaves and two fishes, He will show you a way
to feed thousands.

HORACE BUSHNELL

*The L*ORD *God is a sun and shield;*
   *the L*ORD *bestows favor and honor;*
no good thing does he withhold
   from those whose walk is blameless.
*O L*ORD *Almighty,*
   blessed is the man who trusts in you.

PSALM 84:11–12

You may trust the Lord too little, but you can
never trust Him too much.

ANONYMOUS

*I trust in you, O L*ORD*;*
  I say, "You are my God."
My times are in your hands;
    deliver me from my enemies
    and from those who pursue me.
Let your face shine on your servant;
    save me in your unfailing love.

PSALM 31:14–16

*Trust in the L*ORD *with all your heart*
    and lean not on your own understanding;
in all your ways acknowledge him,
    and he will make your paths straight.

PROVERBS 3:5–6

Laugh Lots and
Rejoice Religiously!

DON'T TAKE YOURSELF TOO *seriously. It just makes life all the harder. It'll all come out in the wash anyway, because God's glory eventually will eclipse everything that goes wrong on this earth. Lighten up and learn to laugh at yourself. None of us is infallible. We make mistakes in life, and more often than not, they're funny. Sometimes, being your own source of comedy is the most fun of all.*

LUCI SWINDOLL

*I delight greatly in the LORD;
    my soul rejoices in my God.*

ISAIAH 61:10

*Jesus said, "I will
see you again and
you will rejoice, and
no one will take
away your joy."*

JOHN 16:22

Clap your hands, all you nations;
shout to God with cries of joy.
How awesome is the LORD Most High,
the great King over all the earth!

PSALM 47:1–2

Since we have been justified through faith,
we have peace with God through our
Lord Jesus Christ, through whom we
have gained access by faith into this grace
in which we now stand. And we rejoice
in the hope of the glory of God.

ROMANS 5:1–2

WORSHIP THE LORD
WITH GLADNESS;
COME BEFORE HIM
WITH JOYFUL SONGS.

PSALM 100:2

Sing to God, sing praise
to his name.
extol him who rides
on the clouds—
his name is the LORD—
and rejoice before him.

PSALM 68:4

I will rejoice in the LORD,
*   I will be joyful in God my Savior.*
The Sovereign LORD is my strength;
*   he makes my feet like the feet of a deer,*
*   he enables me to go on the heights.*

HABAKKUK 3:18

Some people live with a low-grade anxiety
tugging at their spirit all day long. They go
to sleep with it, wake up with it, carry it
around at home, in town, to church, and
with friends. Here's a remedy: Take the
present moment and find something to
laugh at.

People who laugh, last.

BARBARA JOHNSON

*God will
yet fill your
mouth with
laughter
and your lips
with shouts
of joy.*

JOB 8:21

God has brought me laughter.

GENESIS 21:6

*Our mouths were filled with laughter,
    our tongues with songs of joy.
Then it was said among the nations,
    "The Lord has done great things for them."*

PSALM 126:2

*This is the day the Lord has made;
    let us rejoice and be glad in it.*

PSALM 118:24

A happy heart makes
the face cheerful.

PROVERBS 15:13

Let the heavens rejoice, let the earth be glad;
let the sea resound, and all that is in it;
let the fields be jubilant, and everything in them.
Then all the trees of the forest will sing for joy.

PSALM 96:11–12

Be glad and rejoice with me.

PHILIPPIANS 2:18

Every day now I take joy —by refusing to be normal, by refusing to accept the lie that I have to feel miserable about the baggage, the stuff, the sickness, that trails me no matter how I try to hide or outwit it. I choose to do zany, kooky, and funny things to make myself and others laugh.

BARBARA JOHNSON

Some of my friends think of God as a head honcho who sits on a big throne and orders people to "be good." I used to think of God that way too. But I have learned that God wants us to have fun! He created a beautiful world for us, and he created fun. It's all part of the great life he wants us to have. When I find my joy in God, my friends will see it. And maybe they'll want that joy too!

CARISSA SMITH

It is pleasing to our dear God whenever you rejoice or laugh from the bottom of your heart.

MARTIN LUTHER

A Great Big Thanks

OUR CAPACITY TO FEEL, *to think, and to experience is so great—to taste the sweetness of joy that life can bring, to bask in the peace of God, to worship on the mountaintops, to ride high on loving and being loved. All of these are wonderful and precious gifts, and I'm so thankful for them as I journey through this earthly life.*

KATHY TROCCOLI

Give thanks to the LORD for his unfailing love
and his wonderful deeds for men,
for he satisfies the thirsty
and fills the hungry with good things.

PSALM 107:8-9

Ascribe to the LORD the glory due his name;
worship the LORD in the splendor of his
holiness.

PSALM 29:2

How good it is to sing praises to God,
how pleasant and fitting to praise him!

PSALM 147:1

SINCE WE ARE RECEIVING
A KINGDOM THAT CANNOT
BE SHAKEN, LET US BE
THANKFUL, AND SO
WORSHIP GOD ACCEPTABLY
WITH REVERENCE AND AWE.

HEBREWS 12:28

Thanks be to God, who always
leads us in triumphal procession
in Christ and through us
spreads everywhere the
fragrance of the
knowledge of him.

2 CORINTHIANS 2:14

Shout for joy to the LORD, all the earth....
Enter his gates with thanksgiving
and his courts with praise;
give thanks to him and praise his name.
For the LORD is good and his love endures
forever; his faithfulness continues
through all generations.

PSALM 100:1, 4–5

Many, O LORD my God,
are the wonders you have done.
The things you planned for us
no one can recount to you;
were I to speak and tell them,
they would be too many to declare.

PSALM 40:5

Glory in his holy
name; let the hearts of
those who seek the
LORD rejoice.
Look to the LORD
and his strength;
seek his face always.
Remember the wonders
he has done,
his miracles, and
the judgments he
pronounced.
PSALM 105:3–5

Sing to the LORD, sing praises to him,
tell of all his wonderful acts.

1 CHRONICLES 16:9

Lord, make me increasingly aware that to be
chosen by you also includes your choices of
those who nurture me in ways too many and
magnificent for me to imagine. The feast at
which I am sitting is more luxurious than I
can comprehend. My simple table blessing is
inadequate, but ... thank you.

JOY MACKENZIE

Ascribe to the LORD the glory due his name.
Bring an offering and come before him;
worship the LORD in the splendor of his
holiness.

1 CHRONICLES 16:29

Give thanks in all circumstances, for this is
God's will for you in Christ Jesus.

1 THESSALONIANS 5:18

Be on the lookout for God's gifts. The more we

look for them, the more of them we will see.

Better to lose count while naming your bless-

ings than to lose your blessings while counting

your troubles.

AUTHOR UNKNOWN

*Give thanks to the L*ORD*, for he is good;*
  his love endures forever.

1 CHRONICLES 16:34

Just as you received Christ Jesus
as Lord, continue to live in him,
rooted and built up in him,
strengthened in the faith as
you were taught, and overflowing
with thankfulness.

COLOSSIANS 2:6–7

*Praise the L*ORD*.*
*I will extol the L*ORD *with all my heart*
  in the council of the upright and in the
  assembly.
*Great are the works of the L*ORD*;*
  they are pondered by all who delight in them.

PSALM 111:1–2

Me, Myself, and God

WHEN GOD DESCRIBES THE *depth of his feelings for his people and tells us who we are in Christ, he uses tender language, as a parent with a child. Psalm 139 is a good example of how much the Lord thinks of his people.*

This verse shows that God's loving involvement with our lives starts long before birth. Nothing can escape God's concern, according to this psalm—no person, no thought, no place, and no time.

We cannot escape the fact that God cares for us deeply as a parent does for his or her child. How wonderful for us to "hear" his thoughts for his people through Scripture.

You created my inmost being;
*   you knit me together in my mother's womb.*
I praise you because I am fearfully and won-
*   derfully made;*
*   your works are wonderful, I know that full*
*   well.*
My frame was not hidden from you
*   when I was made in the secret place.*
When I was woven together in the depths of
*   the earth,*
*   your eyes saw my unformed body.*
All the days ordained for me were written
*   in your book*
*   before one of them came to be.*

PSALM 139:13–16

Jesus said, "Whoever does God's will is my brother and sister and mother."

MARK 3:35

God created man in his own image,
in the image of God he created him;
male and female he created them.

GENESIS 1:27

You are all sons of the
light and sons of the day.

1 THESSALONIANS 5:5

How great is the love the
Father has lavished on us,
that we should be called
children of God! And that
is what we are!

1 JOHN 3:1

> *"BEFORE I FORMED
> YOU IN THE WOMB I
> KNEW YOU,
> BEFORE YOU WERE
> BORN I SET YOU
> APART," SAYS
> THE LORD.*

JEREMIAH 1:5

God is the only one who knows everything about us. He knows our good thoughts and the thoughts that we struggle to admit even to ourselves. So no matter what you could tell someone else about your life that would change that person's opinion of you, nothing you could say would dampen God's heart toward you.

He knows it all, and he loves you. Surely, this kind of security should set us free to be who we really are.

SHEILA WALSH

*O LORD, you have searched me
   and you know me.
You know when I sit and when I rise;
   you perceive my thoughts from afar.
You discern my going out and my lying down;
   you are familiar with all my ways. ...
Such knowledge is too wonderful for me,
   too lofty for me to attain.*

PSALM 139:1–3, 6

The LORD searches every heart and understands every motive behind the thoughts. If you seek him, he will be found by you.

1 CHRONICLES 28:9

Don't you know that you
yourselves are God's temple
and that God's Spirit lives in you?

1 CORINTHIANS 3:16

Let the Lord have his complete way with you. He loves you so much and has far greater plans for you than you can ever have for yourself. And he does make everything beautiful in his time. Allow God to move in you powerfully. Yield to his voice—calling deeper—higher still. He will take you there.

KATHY TROCCOLI

*LORD, you have assigned me my portion and my cup;
you have made my lot secure.*

PSALM 16:5

By day the Lord directs his love,
at night his song is with me—
a prayer to the God of my life.

PSALM 42:8

You also were included in Christ when you heard the word of truth, the gospel of your salvation. Having believed, you were marked in him with a seal, the promised Holy Spirit, who is a deposit guaranteeing our inheritance until the redemption of those who are God's possession—to the praise of his glory.

EPHESIANS 1:13–14

Where There's a Will ...

THE BIBLE ENCOURAGES US *to devote ourselves to God and to his will for our lives. In light of his mercy, which justifies and sanctifies us, we are to offer ourselves as living sacrifices to him.*

By doing so, we acknowledge God's leadership in our lives. We put aside our selfish desires and misguided ambitions as we strive to align ourselves with God's will.

Once this act of total commitment occurs, our talents and dreams will be surrendered to his purpose. And the more we give ourselves to his will, the more he will bless us and use us.

> Jesus said, "Our Father in heaven, hallowed be your name, your kingdom come, your will be done, on earth as it is in heaven."
>
> MATTHEW 6:9–10

The world and its desires pass away, but the man who does the will of God lives forever.

1 JOHN 2:17

> "STAND AT THE CROSSROADS
> AND LOOK; ASK FOR THE
> ANCIENT PATHS, ASK WHERE
> THE GOOD WAY IS, AND
> WALK IN IT,
> AND YOU WILL FIND
> REST FOR YOUR SOULS,"
> SAYS THE LORD.
>
> JEREMIAH 6:16

Anyone who runs ahead and does not continue in the teaching of Christ does not have God; whoever continues in the teaching has both the Father and the Son.

2 JOHN 9

Teach me to do your will,
for you are my God.

PSALM 143:10

Abraham did not waver through unbelief
regarding the promise of God, but was
strengthened in his faith and gave glory to
God, being fully persuaded that God had
power to do what he had promised.

ROMANS 4:20–21

Jesus prayed, "Father,
if you are willing, take
this cup from me; yet
not my will, but
yours be done."

LUKE 22:42

I desire to do your will, O my God;
your law is within my heart.

PSALM 40:8

God's choice of people to do his will on earth
frequently seemed unusual. He chose Biblical
figures such as Jacob, Abel, Esau, and
Ephraim—flawed characters who didn't appear
to be "religious leaders."

But we can't find fault with those who were
selected to carry out His will. We know so lit-
tle compared with God's infinite understand-
ing of His plans for us.

His will be done.

Jesus said, "If you obey my
commands, you will remain in
my love, just as I have obeyed
my Father's commands and
remain in his love. I have told
you this so that my joy may be in
you and that your joy may be complete."

JOHN 15:10–11

As you graduate you'll probably hear a lot and think a lot about "God's will for your life." Many times we think that means that there is this one perfect plan for our life and if we don't figure it out somehow, we won't be in "God's will." We can be thankful that this is NOT true. There are lots of choices you can make that will please God. What he really wants from you is your worship, your love, and your obedience. If you do those things, all the other details will fall into place.

Jesus said, "If you remain in me and my words remain in you, ask whatever you wish, and it will be given you. This is to my Father's glory, that you bear much fruit, showing yourselves to be my disciples."

JOHN 15:7–8

Jesus said, "All authority in heaven and on earth has been given to me. Therefore go and make disciples of all nations, baptizing them in the name of the Father and of the Son and of the Holy Spirit, and teaching them to obey everything I have commanded you. And surely I am with you always, to the very end of the age."

MATTHEW 28:18–20

Jesus said, "Love the Lord your God with all your heart and with all your soul and with all your mind. This is the first and greatest commandment. And the second is like it: Love your neighbor as yourself."

MATTHEW 22:37–39

The will of God will never take you where the grace of God cannot keep you.

AUTHOR UNKNOWN

Rest, Renew, Reflect

LIFE CAN DRAIN US *of our energy. It can con-*
fuse our sense of what is right and what is
true. But there is a way to re-charge and to
clear away the doubts. Focus on God, not with
a great effort of concentration, but in quiet
and stillness. He will give you strength and
make clear His will for you.

"I will refresh the weary
and satisfy the faint,"
says the LORD.

JEREMIAH 31:25

Jesus said, "Come with me
by yourselves to a quiet
place and get some rest."

MARK 6:31

There remains ... a Sabbath-rest for
the people of God; for anyone who enters
God's rest also rests from his own work, just
as God did from his. Let us, therefore, make
every effort to enter that rest.

HEBREWS 4:9–11

A HEART AT PEACE
GIVES LIFE TO THE BODY.

PROVERBS 14:30

Be still, and know
that I am God.

PSALM 46:10

Jesus said, "Come to me, all you who are
weary and burdened, and I will give you rest.
Take my yoke upon you and learn from me,
for I am gentle and humble in heart, and you
will find rest for your souls. For my yoke is
easy and my burden is light."

MATTHEW 11:28–30

Be at rest once more, O my soul,
*for the L*ORD* has been good to you.*

PSALM 116:7

I will lie down and sleep in peace,
*for you alone, O L*ORD*, make me dwell in*
safety.

PSALM 4:8

Jesus said, "Peace I leave
with you; my peace I
give you. I do not give to
you as the world gives.
Do not let your hearts be
troubled and do not be afraid."

JOHN 14:27

At times, it could flood in! Here are three ways to handle stress, to renew yourself, and to let God into your life:

1. Be gentle. Someone has likened a person under the effects of stress to a car in which the driver has one foot on the gas pedal and one foot on the brake. Be gentle, with yourself and others!

2. Trust God. Our Lord faced stressful circumstances on several occasions, but all of these were minor compared with the stress he endured from Gethsemane to the cross. He understands and will help you through difficult times.

3. Live ethically. How much stress is caused by fear of being found out? Ethical people experience less stress.

We need rest in the Lord, away from other people and pressing concerns, for our bodies as well as for our minds.

You are to rest from trying to make yourself acceptable to God. If you have accepted Christ as Savior, you are as righteous and acceptable in God's eyes today as you will be when you enter his very presence in heaven. God treats you today and forever according to the merits and mediation of the Cross, not your behavior. You are already pleasing God. You are already holy and blameless in his eyes. Your actions may not always measure up to your identity, but you are called a child of God forever. You can cease from any works of self-righteousness.

Living and working in the strength and power of your talents and abilities will only take you so far. It is a long, uphill climb that leads to eventual exhaustion and burnout. But living according to the Spirit will bring you into the green pastures and beside the still waters of the Good Shepherd. "For it is God who works in you to will and to act according to his good purpose" (Philippians 2:13).

That takes the strain off, doesn't it? That infuses the very power of God into your every thought, word, and deed. God is responsible for you. He saved you. He began a good work in you. He will complete it. Surely you are to obey, but you have the power of God to accomplish all that he has planned for your life.

Enter the rest of God by placing your trust in the finished work of the Cross. Commit your way to him. This is the way of success, endurance, and cherished rest for your innermost being. It is the rest of confident faith in the faithfulness of God.

184

CHARLES STANLEY

The LORD tends his flock like a shepherd:
  He gathers the lambs in his arms
and carries them close to his heart;
  he gently leads those that have young.

ISAIAH 40:11

LORD, you establish peace for us;
  all that we have accomplished you have
  done for us.

ISAIAH 26:12

This is what the Sovereign LORD, the Holy One
  of Israel, says:
  "In repentance and rest is your salvation,
  in quietness and trust is your strength."

ISAIAH 30:15

*"Whoever listens to me will live in safety
and be at ease, without fear of harm," says
the Lord.*

PROVERBS 1:33

*The fruit of righteousness will be peace;
the effect of righteousness will be quietness and confidence forever.*

ISAIAH 32:17

*The Lord gives strength to the weary
and increases the power of the weak.
Even youths grow tired and weary,
and young men stumble and fall;
but those who hope in the Lord
will renew their strength.
They will soar on wings like eagles;
they will run and not grow weary,
they will walk and not be faint.*

ISAIAH 40:29–31

*The fear of the Lord leads to life:
Then one rests content, untouched by
trouble.*

PROVERBS 19:23

The mind

controlled by

the Spirit is

life and peace.

ROMANS 8:6

Do not be anxious about anything, but in everything, by prayer and petition, with thanksgiving, present your requests to God. And the peace of God, which transcends all understanding, will guard your hearts and your minds in Christ Jesus.

PHILIPPIANS 4:6–7

In the first chapter of Genesis, the Bible details how, in six days, God created everything from cotton-candy clouds, snails, and monster surf at Sunset Beach, to the whiskered walrus, Venus fly trap, and lightning bolts. And on the seventh day he took a breather. "God blessed the seventh day and made it holy, because on it he rested from all the work of creating that he had done."

Jesus often did the same by retreating with his disciples to a sanctuary, a hiding place, where they could release their heavy loads of anxiety, strengthen their slender threads of patience and, most of all, remember their heavenly Father. As head of the church, Jesus Christ has called for us to take weekly breathers—to rest up, to celebrate ... and to remember.

S. RICKLY CHRISTIAN

*Because of the L*ORD*'s great love we are not*
consumed,
for his compassions never fail.
They are new every morning; great is your
faithfulness.

LAMENTATIONS 3:22–23

May God himself, the God of peace, sanctify
you through and through.

1 THESSALONIANS 5:23

*Cast your cares on the L*ORD
and he will sustain you;
he will never let the righteous fall.

PSALM 55:22

"My Presence will go with you, and
*I will give you rest," says the L*ORD.

EXODUS 33:14

Find rest, O my soul, in God alone;
my hope comes from him.

PSALM 62:5

*He who dwells in the shelter of the Most High
will rest in the shadow of the Almighty.*

PSALM 91:1

*We would be better Christians if we spent
more time alone, and we would actually
accomplish more if we attempted less and
spent more time in isolation and quiet
waiting upon God. The world has become
too much a part of us, and we are afflicted
with the idea that we are not accomplishing anything unless we are always busily
running back and forth.*

*In these hectic days, we should often give
our mind a "Sunday," a time in which it
will do no work but instead will simply be
still, look heavenward, and spread itself
before the Lord.*

L.B. COWMAN

*It is good to wait quietly
for the salvation of the LORD.*

LAMENTATIONS 3:26

"My people will live in peaceful
dwelling places, in secure homes, in
undisturbed places of rest," says the LORD.

ISAIAH 32:18

The LORD makes me lie down in green pastures,
he leads me beside quiet waters,
he restores my soul.

PSALM 23:2–3

The LORD your God is with you,
he is mighty to save.
He will take great delight in you,
he will quiet you with his love
he will rejoice over you with singing.

ZEPHANIAH 3:17

For six days, work is to be done,
but the seventh day shall be your
holy day, a Sabbath of rest to the LORD.

EXODUS 35:2

Several years ago I read a story that often comes to mind when I think about the wisdom of taking life slowly.

It seems that some African missionaries had hired a number of native workers to carry their supplies from one village to another. The missionaries, possessed of the American "push-rush-hurry" mentality, verbally prodded their native employees every day to go a little faster and a little farther than they had the day before. Finally, after three days of being pushed and hurried, the native workers sat down and refused to move.

"What in the world is the problem?" the Americans wanted to know. "We have been making excellent time. There's no need to stop here."

"It is not wise to go so rapidly," the spokesman for the native workers explained. "We moved too fast yesterday. Now today we must stop and wait here for our souls to catch up with our bodies."

Don't you love that? What a powerful philosophy!

Pausing for a moment here and there takes a conscious effort, especially at first, but it will eventually become a habit, and the habit will turn into a way of life. In fact, it will most probably become a foundation stone in one's value system because we cannot live fully or wisely without slowing down, without putting on the brakes, without awareness of each moment.

LUCI SWINDOLL

The Art of Forgiveness

IN SPRING TRAINING *of 2001, Gary Sheffield got himself into some serious trouble with Los Angeles Dodgers fans. Although he was under contract to play for the Dodgers, he talked about wanting to be traded. The fans felt betrayed.*

When the team got to Dodger Stadium for the first regular season game of 2001 and Sheffield's name was announced, the fans booed him. They were making him pay for his remarks.

In the sixth inning, he hit a home run.

Suddenly, those same people who had been booing him—well, they instantly forgave him.

This can be a picture of how God forgives us. Our life can be a mess. Sin can clutter our lives to the point that goodness can hardly be found. When that happens, God can't bear to look upon us. If we are in a sinful, unforgiven state, our only relationship with God is one based on judgment.

But if we turn to God and seek his mercy, everything changes. We are given instant forgiveness. We can immediately bask in the glow of his love and grace.

Are you living with the sad results of sin? You need the smile of God's forgiveness in your life. That's infinitely better than the cheers of 40,000 forgiving baseball fans.

THE SPORTS DEVOTIONAL BIBLE

> *FOR AS HIGH AS THE HEAVENS*
> *ARE ABOVE THE EARTH,*
> *SO GREAT IS GOD'S LOVE*
> *FOR THOSE WHO FEAR HIM;*
> *AS FAR AS THE EAST IS*
> *FROM THE WEST,*
> *SO FAR HAS HE REMOVED*
> *OUR TRANSGRESSIONS*
> *FROM US.*
>
> PSALM 103:11–12

Blessed is he
   whose transgressions are forgiven,
   whose sins are covered.
Blessed is the man
   whose sin the Lord does not count against him
   and in whose spirit is no deceit.

PSALM 32:1–2

If we confess our sins,

God is faithful and just

and will forgive us our

sins and purify us from

all unrighteousness.

1 JOHN 1:9

You are a forgiving God,

gracious and compassionate,

slow to anger and abounding in love.

NEHEMIAH 9:17

Who is a God like you,
* who pardons sin and forgives the transgression*
* of the remnant of his inheritance?*
You do not stay angry forever
* but delight to show mercy.*

MICAH 7:18

God has rescued us from the dominion of
darkness and brought us into the kingdom of
the Son he loves, in whom we have redemp-
tion, the forgiveness of sins.

COLOSSIANS 1:13–14

Be Encouraged!

IF YOU'VE EVER FELT like you're never going to make it across the wide expanse between you and your dreams or that your dreams are routinely dismissed , don't get discouraged. The following examples indicate that you're in distinguished company:

- When Samuel F. B. Morse asked Congress for a grant to build a telegraph line between Washington D.C. and Baltimore, he was greeted with suggestions that instead he build "a railroad to the moon."

- Asked by Parliament whether the telephone would be of any use in Britain, the chief engineer of the British Post Office answered, "No, sir. The Americans have need of the telephone, but we do not. We have plenty of messenger boys."

- In 1903, a year before the Wright brothers flew at Kitty Hawk, Professor Simon New comb, a distinguished astronomer, said that flying without a gas bag was impossible, or at least would require the discovery of a new law of nature.

- A week before the Wright brother's flight, the New York Times editorialized on the rival efforts of Samuel Pierpont Langley, who had just achieved flight by an unmanned heavier-than-air craft: "We hope that Professor Langley will not put his substantial greatness as a scientist in further peril by continuing to waste his time and money on further airship experiments. Life is short and he is capable of services to humanity incomparably greater than trying to fly.

- Within three years, the Wrights had an air plane that could fly forty miles an hour for one hundred miles. They offered it to the British Navy. The Admiralty declined, explaining that the "aeroplane" would be of no practical use in the naval service.

> *YOU HEAR, O LORD,*
> *THE DESIRE OF*
> *THE AFFLICTED;*
> *YOU ENCOURAGE THEM,*
> *AND YOU LISTEN TO*
> *THEIR CRY.*
>
> PSALM 10:17

Why are you downcast, O my soul?
Why so disturbed within me?
Put your hope in God,
for I will yet praise him,
my Savior and my God.

PSALM 43:5

For everything that was written in the past
was written to teach us, so that through
endurance and the encouragement of the
Scriptures we might have hope. May the
God who gives endurance and encourage-
ment give you a spirit of unity among
yourselves as you follow Christ Jesus, so
that with one heart and mouth you may
glorify the God and Father of our Lord
Jesus Christ.

ROMANS 15:4-6

May our Lord Jesus Christ
himself and God our Father,
who loved us and by his grace gave us
eternal encouragement and good hope,
encourage your hearts and strengthen
you in every good deed and word.

2 THESSALONIANS 2:16-17

But hope that is seen is no hope at all. Who hopes for what he already has? But if we hope for what we do not yet have, we wait for it patiently.

ROMANS 8:24–25

We know that in all things God works for the good of those who love him, who have been called according to his purpose. ... What, then, shall we say in response to this? If God is for us, who can be against us? He who did not spare his own Son, but gave him up for us all—how will he not also, along with him, graciously give us all things?

ROMANS 8:28, 31–32

I lift up my eyes to the hills—
  where does my help come from?
My help comes from the LORD,
  the Maker of heaven and earth.

PSALM 121:1–2

All You Need is Love

IF I SPEAK IN THE *tongues of men and of angels, but have not love, I am only a resounding gong or a clanging cymbal. If I have the gift of prophecy and can fathom all mysteries and all knowledge, and if I have a faith that can move mountains, but have not love, I am nothing. If I give all I possess to the poor and surrender my body to the flames, but have not love, I gain nothing. Love is patient, love is kind. It does not envy, it does not boast, it is not proud. It is not rude, it is not self-seeking, it is not easily angered, it keeps no record of wrongs. Love does not delight in evil but rejoices with the truth. It always protects, always trusts, always hopes, always perseveres. Love never fails.*

1 CORINTHIANS 13:1–8

Love is the greatest thing that God can give us for it is Himself: and it is the greatest thing we can give God.

JEREMY TAYLOR

This is how we know what
love is: Jesus Christ laid
down his life for us.

1 JOHN 3:16

*ABOVE ALL, LOVE
EACH OTHER DEEPLY,
BECAUSE LOVE COVERS
OVER A MULTITUDE OF SINS.*

1 PETER 4:8

How great is the love the
Father has lavished on us,
that we should be called
children of God! And that
is what we are!

1 JOHN 3:1

*There is no fear in love.
But perfect love drives out fear.*

1 JOHN 4:18

Your love, O LORD, reaches to the heavens,
your faithfulness to the skies.

PSALM 36:5

Jesus said, "Greater love has
no one than this, that he lay
down his life for his friends."

JOHN 15:13

We know and rely on the love God has for
us. God is love. Whoever lives in love lives
in God, and God in him.

1 JOHN 4:16

Praise be to the LORD,
for he showed his wonderful love to me

PSALM 31:21

Because your love is better than life, LORD,
my lips will glorify you.
I will praise you as long as I live,
and in your name I will lift up my hands.

PSALM 63:3–4

This is my prayer: that your love

may abound more and more in

knowledge and depth of insight,

so that you may be able to

discern what is best and may be

pure and blameless until the day

of Christ, filled with the fruit

of righteousness that comes

through Jesus Christ—to the

glory and praise of God.

PHILIPPIANS 1:9–11

Sources

Cross Training: Becoming Your Spiritual Best. Grand Rapids, MI: Zondervan, 1999.

Finding God's Peace & Joy. Grand Rapids, MI: Zondervan, 1999.

Alive 1: Daily Devotions. ©1995 by S. Rickly Christian. Grand Rapids, MI: Zondervan, 1995.

God Always Has a Plan B. ©1999 by New Life Clinics. Grand Rapids, MI: Zondervan, 1999.

God Made Us Just the Way We Are. ©2000 by New Life Clinics. Grand Rapids, MI: Zondervan, 2000.

God's Words of Life for Leaders. Grand Rapids, MI: Zondervan, 1999.

God's Words of Life for Students. Grand Rapids, MI: Zondervan, 2001.

The Life Promises Bible, New International Version. ©2001. Grand Rapids, MI: Zondervan.

The Sports Devotional Bible. Grand Rapids, MI: Zondervan, 2002.

You, God & Real Life: A Survivor's Guide. Grand Rapids, MI: Zondervan, 2001.

At Inspirio we love to hear from you—
your stories, your feedback,
and your product ideas.
Please send your comments to us
by way of e-mail at
icares@zondervan.com
or the address below:

inspirio™

Inspirio
Attn: Inspirio Cares
5300 Patterson Avenue SE
Grand Rapids, MI 49530